J. & W. ATTLEE,

MILLERS,

Maltsters & Corn Dealers,

HIGH STREET,

DORKING.

ALL KINDS OF AGRICULTURAL SEEDS,

HOPS,

English and Foreign Oilcake, &c., &c.

ECONOMICAL HOUSEKEEPING!!

The BEST VALUE for READY MONEY
IN
GROCERIES,
TEAS, COFFEES,
AND
PROVISIONS,

MAY BE OBTAINED AT

The "Golden Canister" Stores,

(FOUR DOORS FROM THE POST OFFICE),

HIGH STREET, DORKING,

OF

ROBERT PEARCE,

SOLE PROPRIETOR OF THE CELEBRATED

"PREMIER TEA,"

(A choice blend of India and China Teas 2s. 8d. per lb.)

AND AGENT FOR THE SALE OF

W. & A. GILBEY'S WINES & SPIRITS,

Bass & Co.'s PALE ALE.   Guinness and Co.'s
DUBLIN STOUT.

THE LEAMINGTON MINERAL WATERS, AND

Huntley and Palmer's Reading Biscuits & Cakes.

Families waited upon Daily.

THE WHITE HORSE

Family & Commercial Hotel,

DORKING.

FRED. COOKE, *Proprietor.*

OMNIBUS OR CARRIAGES AT SOUTH EASTERN & BRIGHTON RAILWAY STATIONS UPON ARRIVAL OF TRAINS.

DORKING COACH OFFICE.

TURNER BROS.,

Carpenters, Builders & Undertakers,

DORKING.

NEW AND SECOND-HAND FURNITURE, CARPET AND BEDDING DEALERS.

GOODS CAREFULLY REMOVED.

Furniture Warehouse: EAST STREET.

Building Works: 5, HAMPSTEAD ROAD, DORKING.

W. M. WOODLAND,

Stone, Slate and Marble Works,

WEST STREET, DORKING.

Monumental and General Masonry executed promptly at Moderate Charges.

ESTABLISHED 1804.

WILLIAM STONESTREET,

CHIMNEY SWEEPER,

CHURCH STREET, DORKING.

ALL KINDS OF FLUES CAREFULLY CLEANED.   *Smoky Chimneys Cured.*

Clean Cloths for Upstairs Apartments.

Work taken by the Year, Half-year, or Job.

All Orders by Post punctually attended to.

J. S. ARTHURS,
WATCHMAKER & JEWELLER,
EAST STREET, DORKING.

After 29 years' experience as a practical workman, J. S. A. guarantees good workmanship, strict promptitude and moderate charges.

HOUSE AND TURRET CLOCKS Wound, and Watches Kept in Repair by the Year.—Terms strictly moderate.

Silver Cups or Articles suitable for Prizes supplied on the shortest notice.	A well-selected Stock of Watches, Plate and Jewellery, all of which are warranted.

J. S. A. begs to intimate that articles left with him are not kept longer than is really necessary for their thorough repair.

Agent for the Commercial Union Fire & Life Assurance Comp.y

AGENT'S.—DAYS FOR CALLING.

MICKLEHAM—Mrs. Hill, the Post Office—FRIDAY.
LEATHERHEAD—Mr. Batten, Church Street FRIDAY.
EFFINGHAM—Mr. J. West, Grocer—FRIDAY.
BROCKHAM—Mr. Streeter, the Green—TUESDAY.
BETCHWORTH—Mr. Saunders, the Post Office—TUESDAY.

LETTERS BY POST PROMPTLY ATTENDED TO.

Established above a Century.

JAS. M. HUBBARD

(Son of the late Thomas Hubbard),

WATCH AND CLOCK MAKER,

HIGH STREET, DORKING.

Church, Turret, and House Clocks attended by the Year. Plate and Jewellery Repaired.

C. WHALEY,
FURNISHING IRONMONGER,
TINMAN,

BRAZIER, BELL HANGER AND GAS FITTER,

WEST STREET, DORKING.

KING,
THE OLD ESTABLISHED FANCY BASKET SHOP,
Near the Public Hall, West Street,
DORKING.

Makers of every kind of Flower and other Baskets.

N.B.—A LARGE ASSORTMENT ALWAYS IN STOCK.

Baskets being Made on the Premises, all Orders will be punctually attended to.

P.S.—OBSERVE THE ADDRESS.

W. BORER,
CORN & SEED MERCHANT,
HIGH STREET, DORKING.

HAY, STRAW, MALT, HOPS, ETC.
LINSEED AND OTHER CAKES.
SPRATT'S FIBRINE AND DOG BISCUITS.

WHITE & SONS,
Auctioneers,
SURVEYORS, GENERAL VALUERS,
ESTATE AND TITHE AGENTS,
DORKING.

THE DORKING SEWING MACHINE DEPOT.

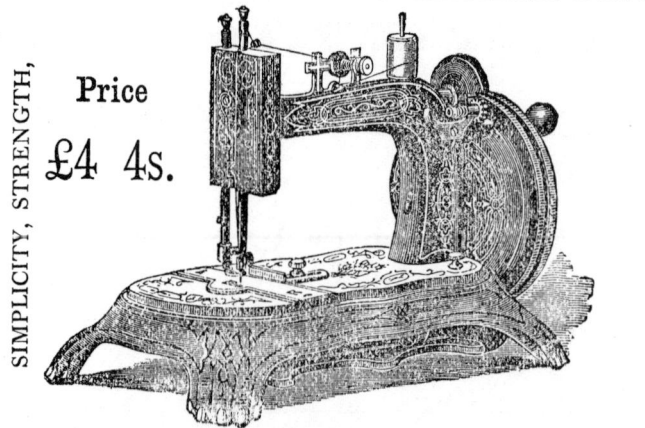

SIMPLICITY, STRENGTH,

Price £4 4s.

BEAUTY AND LIGHT RUNNING.

THE
"HOME COMPANION" Sewing Machine

Is a "Lock-Stitch" which is universally acknowledged to be the only reliable stitch, and for strength, firmness, and durability, it cannot be equalled. The saving of thread as compared with machines making the Chain-Stitch is considerable, where the machine is much used. And we feel confident that, whenever persons wishing to buy Sewing Machines give the "HOME COMPANION" Sewing Machine a fair trial in competition with other Machines.

SOLE AGENT for Dorking: H. KENDALL, High Street.
MACHINES CLEANED AND REPAIRED.

RED LION
FAMILY HOTEL, DORKING.

G. GRAVES

BEGS to announce that he has taken the above well-known first-class Family Hotel, and respectfully informs the Inhabitants of the Town and its vicinity, that his best endeavours will be given to conduct the Business in its various departments, so as to merit the patronage of the Public generally.

As a Family Hotel, the Rooms will be found comfortably furnished. Wines and Spirits of the best qualities only will be supplied, and every attention given so as to ensure the comfort of Visitors.

As Family Wine and Spirit Merchant, every Article supplied will be at lowest possible Prices, according to quality.

In the Yard—Flys, Open Carriages, Pony Carriages, Hunters, Hacks, &c., let on hire at reasonable rates.

WEDDING BREAKFASTS & BALL SUPPERS SUPPLIED.

GOOD BILLIARD ROOM.

A large Assembly Room for Dinner Parties and Entertainments.

HEARSE AND MOURNING COACHES LET ON HIRE.

G. G trusts to receive a liberal share of patronage, and all orders he may be favoured with, will have his prompt and best attention.

REMINISCENCES OF OLD DORKING

by
John Attlee

KOHLER AND COOMBES
DORKING
1977

Attlee's Reminiscences of Old Dorking

John Attlee

Born 13th August 1828, son of Richard & Harriet Attlee of High Street, Dorking, and baptised at St. Martin's. Died 27th December 1913, aged 85.

On March 23rd, 1912, there appeared in the Dorking Advertiser, <u>Reminiscences of Old Dorking</u>, by John Attlee. In 1952, A.W. and W. Eade, the West Street antique dealers, republished this article and others from the same 1912 issue, in a small booklet. The articles on <u>Dorking Changes</u> and <u>Queen Victoria's Jubilee</u> were written by Dorking Advertiser journalists for this issue. Mr. and Mrs. Eade updated some of the information to 1952 by means of useful footnotes; these footnotes have again been revised in this 1977 edition. It must be remembered that John Attlee was writing about the Dorking he knew in the 1840's and 1850's.

> "Possessing a strong and retentive memory, John Attlee had an acquaintance with his native town, its inhabitants and its affairs, such as few others could claim. An excellent raconteur, his recitals of events of half a century ago afforded pleasure to those who were privileged to hear them."

So wrote the Dorking Advertiser in its tribute to John Attlee on his death in 1913, having a year earlier obtained from him the <u>Recollections</u> here re-published.

John Attlee came of a long line of farmers, brewers, millers, agricultural merchants, and with his brother William followed his father into the family business. He took a keen interest in the varied commercial activity of the High Street - where the weekly market was held outside the Attlee's shop door - and its extension along South Street and down West Street. John soon knew everyone.

i

Attlee's Reminiscences of Old Dorking

The <u>Handbook of Dorking</u> (1855 and 1858 - reprinted by Kohler and Coombes, 1974) had carried Richard Attlee's advertisement: "Mealman, Maltster and Corn-dealer, High Street, Dorking". Twenty-five years later J. & W. Attlee were offering their "Tooting Ales and London Porter" to be had at their Stores in the Rotunda, besides "All kinds of Agricultural Seeds, Hops, English & Foreign Oil Cake, &c., &c.," from the High Street premises near the western end of the High Pavement.

Until the turn of the century John Attlee was kept fully occupied in his business. Then he retired, and was able to express his interest and concern for the affairs of Dorking in fresh ways. Among them were membership of the Urban Council, of the Committee of the Cottage Hospital, the Holmwood Common Committee, directorships of the Gas Company, and the Villa Building Company. He had leisure, too, to reflect on the Dorking of his youth, to recall with rare precision the former occupiers of almost every shop and business in the town, identifying premises by their current occupiers and uses. Could such a feat be repeated - now that the inconstant, faceless firm has largely replaced the family who used to live over the shop?

Attlee's Reminiscences of Old Dorking

High Street (north side, corner of North Street)

It is not given to many to be able to carry back their memory to between sixty and seventy years, and to recall events of that period with any great degree of accuracy and completeness. But Mr. John Attlee, who is in the enjoyment of fairly good health, considering his advanced age, is the possessor of a remarkably retentive memory, and he has been good enough to supply us with some of his early recollections of old Dorking.

He can remember, he says, when No. 1, High-street was a barber's shop kept by a man named Harvey;(1) No. 2 was a greengrocer's owned by a man named John Kennis, who had a daughter always known as "Betty Kennis"; No. 3 was a grocer's, kept by a Mr. James King, a native of Ashtead, and No. 4 was a fishmonger's kept by a man named Lovell. No. 5 was a private house, owned by a Mrs. King,(2) whose husband was a maltster. The James King, who lived at No. 3 bought this property and built the present house upon it, retaining the old malthouses as stores. Though of the same name he was no relation of the old maltster. No. 6 was owned and occupied by Mr. John Philps, the grandfather of the present owner and proprietor. This was in two tenements, Mr. Thomas Philps, the father of Mr. John Philps, living in the one nearest the "Wheatsheaf." He lived to a great age, and was married four times. The "Wheatsheaf" was owned by a cousin of Mr. Philps. A Mr. Francis Griffin carried on the business and did well there. His wife was an excellent caterer, and the market dinners were wonderfully good and well attended. He afterwards removed to what is now known as "The Bell" in West-street. The next house to the "Wheatsheaf" was a grocer's kept by a

---

(1) Later Lanhams and Post Office; 1977 Batemans.
(2) 1952 Kinghams; 1977 Seeboard.

Attlee's Reminiscences of Old Dorking

Mr. Philpot. And the next was a chemist's kept by a Mr. Cousins. Adjoining it was a furniture warehouse kept by Mr. William Miller, who was also an auctioneer. Next to that was a private house occupied by Mrs. Cheesman, who died in 1836, and then came another private house, tenanted by Mrs. Meek; she had twin step-daughters, who were exactly alike. The house now occupied by Mr. Spratley was then Mr. Thomas Hubbard's, watch and clock maker. Where Messrs. Kingham's grocery stores are was a cooper's and basket shop, kept by a Quaker named Banks Farrand.(1) Smith's Library was an undertaker's, a Mr. John Niblett being proprietor. A Mr. Matthew Blaker owned and occupied the house where Mr. W. Cole now carries on business. Mr. Blaker was a fellmonger and tanner; his tanyard was in the Mill-lane, where Boxall's brewery now stands. An old house,(2) with small diamond lead casement windows, stood on the site of Messrs. White and Sons' offices. It was a china and crockery shop kept by a person of the name of Spratley. The houses at the other side of the passage leading to the church were old tumbledown tenements, one of which was occupied by the firm of Hooker and Nicholls.(3) The next was formerly the site of Piper and Dewdney's Bank, which failed in 1826. The ironmonger's shop now Pierson and Co. was kept by a Quaker named William Dean. What is now Mackney and Pierce was kept by Mr. Thomas Spokes; he was noted for selling the best of everything at a fair price. A Mr. George Dewdney carried on the business of a harness-maker at the shop now owned by Mr. Curry.

An old member of the Society of Friends, named Robert Trimmer, had a china and glass shop at what is now "The Sun" beerhouse.

---

(1) 1912 Kinghams; 1952 Boots.
(2) 1912 Whites; 1977 (rebuilt) Montague Burton.
(3) 1952 Barclays Bank; 1977 (rebuilt) Barclays Bank.

Attlee's Reminiscences of Old Dorking

The front remains the same as then. "The Three Tuns" inn(1) was kept by a man named Thomas Wellman. The next house was owned by Mr. William Cheesman, who carried on the business of a candle maker and tallow chandler. Formerly corn used to be pitched inside the "Black Horse"(2) for sale, and more business was done in grain than in liquor. The next was a grocer's and pork butcher's shop, carried on by a man named John Adds. A Mr. White owned and occupied the corner house; he built all the cottages at the upper part of Mill-lane. The large private house occupied by Mr. Moorhouse was the residence of Mr. John Philps; he was the owner of the "Wheatsheaf," and of considerable property in the neighbourhood. On the site of the Imperial Club, Messrs. Davey, and Messrs. Hart, Scales, and Hodges' offices, some very old cottages stood.(3) A private house occupied by Mr. Matthew Holden stood where Messrs. Nicklin and Co.'s drapery shop now is. Next was a private house - now a tailor's shop - occupied by Mrs. Dewdney.(4) Messrs. Hart and Son's offices and private residence formed the site of the shops now there. Then comes the private house, now the residence of Mr. Howard, the veterinary surgeon. It was formerly occupied by an independent gentleman, Mr. John Savage. Mr. Philip Cooke owned and lived in the next house,(5) where

---

(1) Three Tuns (demolished); 1952 International Stores; 1977 Etam.
(2) 1913 rebuilt and named Three Tuns; 1977 Tesco.
(3) 1912 Messrs. Davey and Messrs. Hart, Scales & Hodges; 1952 Richard Hicks and Messrs. Hart, Scales & Hodges; 1977 Chevertons and Messrs. Hart, Scales & Hodges.
(4) 1912 tailor's; 1977 Post Office.
(5) 1912 Misses Fuller; 1977 Car Park.

Attlee's Reminiscences of Old Dorking

the Misses Fuller now reside. The next was Mr. Gilliam's, a stonemason. His yard was full of gravestones and monuments. His wife and daughters kept a dame's school for little boys and girls. Between Mr. Gilliam's and the coachbuilder's, some old cottages stood. Mr. Walker built the house next to the coachbuilder's shop. The next house faced due east, and was part of the Shrub Hill estate. Mr. Adams, the old gardener, lived there and his two daughters did a little dressmaking and millinery work. Then there was an open space with a large meadow, and the garden, stables, and coachhouses of Shrub Hill, and just beyond this was the entrance to the nursery grounds(1) of Mr. Robert Westland, who was succeeded by Messrs. Ivery and Son. The last house on that side of the way was the residence of Mr. William Hart, M.R.C.S. He lived there for many years, and had a good practice.

London Road

"Pipp Brook" was the residence of Mr. William Cranford, a very clever man, and a good one too. Mr. John Abel owned Pippbrook Mill, and the land and houses adjoining.

High Street (south side)

The corner house now occupied by Messrs. Lascelles, Tickner and Co. was formerly the residence of Mr. Joseph Moore,(2) an independent gentleman. Shrub Hill,(3) the site of which is now covered with shops, was the residence of the Earl and Countess of Rothes.

---

(1) 1977 Wathen Road corner to Deepdene Car Centre.
(2) 1912 Lascelles; 1952 Lovibonds; 1977 Kentucky Fried Chicken.
(3) 1912 shops; 1952 Dunns the Furriers; 1977 House of Flowers and Glenda Gray.

Attlee's Reminiscences of Old Dorking

Two cottages stood on the site of what is now Messrs. Andrews' music warehouse.(1) The "Surrey Yeoman" was a little old public-house kept by a man named Hull. The baker's and confectioner's shop was kept by a Mr. Jonathan Pullen. He was a very clever man, and a beautiful writer. He used to engross deeds for Messrs. Hart and Sons, the solicitors. One of the adjoining houses was occupied by Mr. Richard Rose, a good man, and highly respected. A Mr. Reeves lived in one of the others. The baker's shop now occupied by Mr. White was formerly a little general shop kept by a Mr. Mitchell. The next house was occupied by Mr. Joseph Balchin, whose wife and her sister had a milliner's shop and traded as Balchin and Penn. Then came a little general shop kept by Mrs. Gittins, whose husband was a whitesmith and was an excellent workman. The "Ram" Inn(2) in the old days always looked wonderfully shabby and neglected. It was the headquarters of one of the clubs, and on Whit-Monday in each year there was the annual feast of the members.

Crossing the road, the corner house was then as now a butcher's shop kept by a man named Alloway, and afterwards by his sons William and Charles. Next was a shop kept by a man named Niblett; he did a little in the pork butchering line and let out a horse or two for hire. Then there was a grocer's shop kept by a Mr. George Robinson. He was a beautiful writer, and after he gave up business the 13th Duke of Norfolk gave him employment which he held till his death. The site is now occupied by Messrs. Attree and Sons' shop. Where Messrs. Down's offices and Mr. W.L. Batson's house now stand, there were some little old cottages, one of which was occupied by an old man named Davy, a fishmonger. His wife was always known as Aunt Hetty. Mr. George Curtis lived in the next house (now part of the "White Horse") before he built the

---

(1) 1912 Andrews; 1952 Robins.
(2) 1977 Acres the bakers and Camelot.

Attlee's Reminiscences of Old Dorking

houses next door. The "White Horse" was kept by Mr. William Penn, who was a lineal descendent of the famous Quaker, the founder of Pennsylvania. The Horsham coach changed horses here. In 1848 Mr. John Goddard succeeded Mr. Penn, and made a fortune there. The little shop next to it was occupied by a chemist and druggist named Paffard. Then came a row of private houses: an old gentleman named Lynn lived in the one now occupied by Mr. Dixon (late Doubleday). Another was the residence of Mr. Thomas Napper, M.R.C.S. The one now a fishmonger's shop was occupied by Mr. E.J.R. Russell, the organist. The site of the Capital and Counties' Bank was formerly a corn dealer's shop, kept by one John Charman; his wife was a clever milliner and dressmaker. The "Red Lion"(1) had a Mr. Coombes as proprietor. The shop now Mr. Bond's,(2) was a baker's, kept by Mr. John Sanders. He let off one large room on the ground floor, where the watchmaker's shop now is, to a solicitor named Martin; he did not stay long in Dorking. Next was a draper's, with Mr. I.R. Overton proprietor. Part of his shop was Messrs. Nash and Neale's Bank, and the cashier divided his time between attending to the bank customers and selling ribbons and calico. A portion of the upper part of the house was occupied by a lady and her two daughters named Pethybridge, who kept a dame's school, where almost all the tradesmen's children went. There was a wide gateway leading into a large yard, where the dyer's shop now stands, for the house was formerly an inn known as the "Bell." Next was a barber's shop, kept by a man named Mills, and afterwards by Mr. Caffyn, and adjoining was a little chandler's and a greengrocer's kept by a Mrs. Chatfield. Then came Mr. Marshall's boot and shoe shop. All these shops had two or three steps to be ascended before they could be entered. But people did not mind a few steps in those days.

---

(1) 1977 new parade of shops (Mansons the butchers to Nationwide Building Society).
(2) 1912 Mr. Bond; 1977 White's (formerly opposite).

Attlee's Reminiscences of Old Dorking

Mr. Lucock's alehouse and brewery(1) was the next. His old ale, which he retailed at 8d. per quart, was famous then. The butcher's shop was formerly a grocer's, kept by Edward Worley; he afterwards had the "Running Horses," Mickleham, where his wife and daughter, by their great industry and good management, made and saved money. The Gas Company's show rooms was a draper's kept by two ladies, Miss Julia Blackburn and Miss Jane Puzey. Next was a confectioner's, Mr. Richard Uwins, who had a name for selling excellent articles. The next house had various tenants, among them Mr. Uwins, jun., who sold music. What is now Mr. Warner's bootshop was a draper's, kept by Mr. William Latter, and Mr. Beetham Wilson's was a candle-maker's and tallow chandler's, Mr. George Eives being the proprietor. Where Messrs. Kingham and Co.'s wine and spirit stores are was formerly an old house occupied by Mr. Thos. Hubbard, jun., watch and clockmaker. Mr. Robert Best Ede had the next house.(2) He was a very clever maker of scents and was chemist to Queen Victoria. He was also a printer and employed a large number of hands. He also had the Post Office. He died in 1845. What is now Stone and Turner's ironmongery shop was formerly S. Fuller and Son, then Ward and Niblett, afterwards Ward, and subsequently P.L. Saubergue. Next door was Mr. Robert Dewdney's hat shop. Mr. Charles Colgate(3) had part of the shop now Mr. Mason's, and Miss Isard that nearest the Chequers Yard as a toy shop. Mr. Colgate did a good business, and Miss Isard's was patronised by the ladies of the neighbourhood. The house now occupied by the London County and Westminster Bank was the residence of a gentleman named Pitt; afterwards Mr. W. Chaldecott, M.R.C.S., lived there for many years.

---

(1) 1952 Freeman, Hardy & Willis.
(2) 1952 Clarke (chemist); 1977 Gorge Restaurant.
(3) 1912 Masons; 1977 Robert Dyas (late Stone & Turner, formerly Saubergue) removed from site of Sainsburys.

Attlee's Reminiscences of Old Dorking

Where Messrs. Cheesman and Bromley's shop now stands was a private house, the residence of Mrs. Attlee.

The next is Messrs. J. and W. Attlee's,(1) millers and corn merchants; it was formerly kept by the late Mr. Richard Attlee, and previously by Mr. John Attlee, his father. The business is one of the oldest in the town, and has been carried on by four generations. The next house was a barber's shop, and then came a dressmaker's, Miss Gittins. William Broad, the last of the old Dorking coachmen, lived in the house now occupied by Messrs. F. Parfitt and Son. A man named Martyr carried on the business of a butcher where Messrs. George Peters and Son now are. The "Bull's Head" was kept by Joseph Woodroffe; a great many coaches stopped and changed horses there.

Pump Corner

In the corner house now occupied by the Misses Gumbrell, the milliners, Messrs. R. and W. Marsh carried on the business of clothiers and outfitters. Mr. John Brown, baker and confectioner, had the business now carried on by Messrs. Wickham and Son.(2)

South Street (north-west side)

"The White Lion" (now closed),(3) was kept by Mrs. Spratley. Mr. W. Beckett, tailor, had the shop in South-street where Mr. G.M. Boorer, tobacconist, now lives. The next

---

(1) 1912 J. & W. Attlee; 1952 National Provincial Bank; 1977 vacant.
(2) 1912 Wickham; 1952 Loyns; 1977 Sirrons Employment Agency and Pump Corner Antiques.
(3) 1912 closed; 1952 Eastmans (cleaners); 1977 R. Palladine (tailor).

Attlee's Reminiscences of Old Dorking

house was occupied by Mr. Frederick Muggeridge, architect and surveyor. The next was a private house where Mrs. Cheesman(3) lived; she had previously carried on the business of a wine and spirit merchant for many years. The old established grocer's shop, now Messrs. Coles and Adams', was formerly Mr. John Norman's. A row of pollarded lime trees stood in front, which added greatly to the beauty of the old town. The next house had various tenants. Then came a corn dealer's shop kept by Mr. James Wells. A marine store dealer's was the next, proprietor, Richard Skilton. The greengrocer's business now carried on by Messrs. Croucher was formerly Mr. Thomas Howard's; he left it and went to the Deepdene as gamekeeper. The old tumbledown cottage next to it was occupied by a very tall, thin man named Thomas Upfold. "The Spotted Dog" was opened as a beershop soon after the passing of the Duke of Wellington's Beer Act. The next was the Brewery House, owned and occupied by Mr. James Cheesman; the brewery was at the back of it. A confectioner named John Hubbard had a shop next door. A picturesque old cottage,(1) where a man named James Taylor lived, occupied part of the site of what is now the Post Office. Where the Junction-road is now there was a large garden. The private house next to Messrs. Bargman's office was the residence of an old lady, a Mrs. Skipper. Next was a harness maker, Mr. Jonathan Edwards; an excellent workman. The small houses adjoining had various occupants. The large house next to them was the residence of Mr. John Adee Curtis, a surgeon.(2) A school for young ladies, kept by the Misses Stent and Sumner, occupied the house now the offices of Messrs.

---

(1) 1912 Post Office and Council Offices; 1952 Seeboard and Dorking Bookshop; 1977 Websters Bookshop.
(2) 1952 Tanners (printers); 1977 Reynolds and Dorking Tyre Service, Dorking Advertiser offices above.
(3) 1912 Degenhardt's; 1977 Degenhardt's.

Attlee's Reminiscences of Old Dorking

Colls and Sons. Then came a private house occupied and belonging to Mr. Thomas Harbroe, and the adjoining house was a small grocer's shop kept by Mrs. Sayers. The private house next to it was the residence of Mr. Richard Clapton, an independent old gentleman. The Tithe Barn(1) adjoining was formerly in Church-street. It was used when the tithes were taken in kind. The Tithe Commutation Act was passed in the year 1836. A little wooden building that stood next was a butcher's shop, kept by Mr. Joseph Fuller, who did an excellent business there. The cage, or lock-up, stood where Mr. Tracy's shop now is. The workhouse(2) was a little distance behind; an old man named Beecham was the Master. "The Old House," where Dr. Cornish now resides, was formerly the residence of Mr. James Bravery. He used Westcott Mill, and did a considerable business. The mill was burnt down on the 8th of January, 1843, and Mr. Bravery dropped down dead in the old stable close by on the 13th of the same month. The new mill erected on the site of the old one is now unused, and stands empty. Where Mr. Shearburn's house now stands was a large nursery garden.(3) The house where Mr. Chalcraft lives was formerly the residence of Mr. Ryde. The small houses adjoining had various tenants. The next large house was the residence of Mrs. Walters, and that adjoining was the house and workshops of Mr. Edward Walker, a carpenter and builder, and a first rate workman. Trellis Cottage was occupied by two old ladies and their brother. On the site of the house known as St. Margaret's stood a thatched cottage.(4) A Miss Puttock lived there and let apartments.

---

(1) 1977 Haybarn House (offices and vacant shop).
(2) 1912 Mr. Tracy and Methodist Church; 1977 new offices (vacant).
(3) 1912 Shearburn; 1977 Adlard's Bartholemew Press.
(4) 1912 St. Margaret's; 1977 Harmer's Autos.

Attlee's Reminiscences of Old Dorking

South Street (south-east side)

On the opposite side of the road there were some little low cottages, with no upstair rooms, and a dwarf wall in front of them. These were the last houses in that road. Next to them came the two tall semi-detached houses which are still standing; these were built from the materials of Lord Nelson's house at Merton. After his death his residence was pulled down, and the building materials sold. Mr. Dendy (the then owner of the land on which the houses now stand) bought a large quantity of doors and windows very cheap, and built these two houses with them. A Mrs. Fuller lived in one, and Mr. John Bull (the first registrar of births, marriages and deaths under the Act of 1837), in the other. Next is Townfield(1); this was the residence of Mr. John G. Stillwell. At the entrance to it, and where the tall trees stand, there was formerly a grocer and baker's shop, kept by Mr. Beckett. "The Queen's Head" was originally a private house, but was turned into a public; Mr. Daniels kept it. The old house where Mr. Batson now lives is very little altered.(2) The Rev. George Feachem, the vicar, lived there till his death in 1837. The cottage residence next was a boarding school kept by a Mr. Wills. The road to Rose Hill comes between this and the next house, which was formerly the residence of Mr. W. Shearburn, and recently that of his grandson, Mr. W. Shearburn. The next old house was the residence of Mr. John Rudge, and the next was that of Mr. Powis, who assisted Mr. R.B. Ede in his manufacture of scents. Mr. Rudge had a malthouse adjoining. Then came the beershop known as "The Cricketers." The old-fashioned residence adjoining was a school for young ladies,(3) kept by Miss Cobden and Miss Mitchell. The Misses Duncumb lived in the house (now pulled down) opposite the Wesleyan Church.

---

(1) 1977 Falkland Road corner to Bus Station and forecourt.
(2) 1912 Mr. Batson; 1952 Mays Garage.
(3) 1977 Little Dudley House Restaurant.

Attlee's Reminiscences of Old Dorking

"Holder House,"(1) next to it, had a row of lime trees in front of it. It was the residence of a gentleman named Trollope.
Mr. Arthur Dendy owned and lived at "Stapleton."(2) Mrs. Whitehouse, the widow of the Congregational Minister, lived in one of the old houses where Victoria-terrace now stands; John Bradley in the other. The cottages opposite "Wyngates" were occupied by Richard Finch, commonly known as "Lord Finch," and George Tooley respectively. Tooley's wife was a dressmaker. Mr. John Beckett lived in the house occupying the site of Miss Spratley's toy and news shop.(3) Rose Hill House was the residence of a gentleman named Lowndes. About the year 1793 old Louis Phillippe (afterwards King of France) occupied it for a time. About the year 1837 Mr. Lowndes sold the property to Mr. Newland, who turned the residence into two tenements, cut up the land into building plots, and made the road round Rose Hill.

West Street (north side, going down)

The corner house in West-street, now a draper's shop, was formerly an old inn known as the "Queen's Arms."(4) There was a gateway leading into a large yard, and round the house was a gallery like that of the old inns in the Borough, so graphically described by Dickens in "Pickwick Papers." Part of the old inn was occupied by a man named Baverstock; he was a cooper by trade, and

---

(1) 1952 Sub-Post Office to Andrews (music shop); 1977 Sub-Post Office to Mid-Surrey Antiques.
(2) 1952 Co-op; 1977 new shops below P.D.S.A. offices.
(3) 1919 after road-widening War Memorial to Bandstand; 1977 War Memorial and garden.
(4) 1912 draper's; 1952 Midland Bank to Dorking Foundry; 1977 Midland Bank to Dorking Museum.

Attlee's Reminiscences of Old Dorking

got a good living at it. The next house was Mr. Bartlett's, a blacksmith; the large blacksmith's shop stood next, and a great many horses were shod there. The house now occupied by Mr. Allatson was formerly Mr. Rayme's. He came into considerable property in the Isle of Wight, and retired from the business, which he disposed of to a Mr. William Rudge. Then came a cottage tenanted by one Joseph Lindsay,(1) who looked after Broad's coachhorses. Adjoining was a laundry kept by Mrs. Farley and her daughters. What is now the "Bell" Inn was formerly the "Star," and was kept by a man named Potter. The baker's shop next to it was kept by a man named Murphy. In front of the West-street Chapel there formerly stood a house; it was pulled down about the year 1834.

West Street (south side, going down)

At the top of West-street, on the left-hand side, were some disreputable old cottages, and then a few better ones, and where Mr. Adams' two shops now stand there was a grass plot with a path leading to the Friends' Meeting House(2) behind it, which still remains and is used as a warehouse. What is now Mr. H. Fuller's butcher's shop was occupied by a man named Lynn, who disposed of the property to Mr. John Fuller, the grandfather of the present owner. A new and secondhand furniture warehouse, owned by a greatly-respected man named Joseph Sayers, occupied the site of the present fishmonger's shop. The workshops were behind, and are now used by Messrs. Sherlock, the coach-builders. What were until recently the Friary and Holroyd's offices was formerly a cook's shop.(3) Mrs. Smith, the harness maker's, was a clothier's. The little low cottage

---

(1) 1952 Tarling's Music Shop; 1977 Eleanor Hutton.
(2) 1912 Adams; 1977 Scott Hudson.
(3) 1912 Friary Offices; 1952 A.W. and W. Eade Antiques; 1977 Old House (antiques).

Attlee's Reminiscences of Old Dorking

next was occupied by a man named Dale, a very clever gardener. His son emigrated to America, and is now the proprietor of one of the largest nursery grounds in New York. The other little cottages were tenanted by labourers. The house with bay windows and the yard was owned and occupied by Mr. Samuel Bothwell, a builder.(1) The next had Mr. Samuel Reeves, a watch and clock maker, for a tenant. Where the Temperance Hotel now is, was a butcher's shop kept by Mr. George King, and a large yard with stables occupied the site of the lower part of Junction-road, and the shops of Messrs. Moore and Weller, the old carrier, James Razzell, living opposite on the site of their other shop. "The Old House at Home" was formerly only a cottage. The Rev. John Wesley's old coachman lived in one of the old cottages at the back of it, and Elizabeth Bird, miller, lived in another; she had the Rookery Mill, Westcott. Where the Town Hall now stands, there was formerly a plumber, painter and glazier's shop, kept by John Fuller and Richard Botting.(2) Clarendon House was tenanted by Mrs. Bird, who let apartments. The two semi-detached houses were occupied by Mr. Sturgeon and Mr. Stratton. Where the Howard-road now is some tall trees stood, and there was a large meadow. What is now the Vicarage was formerly known as "Sondes Place." It was once the residence of and was owned by Earl Sondes. It stood empty for a time previous to 1837; it was then purchased for a vicarage.

West Street (north side, going up)

Opposite stood a farm yard, with a barn, a cow-stall and other buildings. A

---

(1) 1952 Mr. Atkinson; 1977 West Street House Antiques.
(2) 1912 Town Hall; 1952 Fire Station; 1977 County Library Store.

Attlee's Reminiscences of Old Dorking

Mr. Thomas Stent lived where Mr. George White and his sisters now reside. A Mrs. Smith and her daughter lived in the next house; these houses and the next, where Mr. Richard Chitty used to live, have not been altered at all. The stuccoed residence, now the High School, was formerly a nice-looking brick-built house(1) with trained pear trees growing on each side of the front door. It was called "The Parsonage House," and was let on a long lease with "Parsonage Mill" and Parsonage Farm, to a Mr. Richard Greaves, who also had Bradley Farm. He died in 1836, and was succeeded by his son, who died in 1839. Corn stacks and hay ricks stood on the right hand side of the road now leading to the S.E. railway station. On the site of the "Star" Inn was a blacksmith's shop, where waggon and cart wheels were re-tyred. Going up West-street, and next to the blacksmith's, there were two or three little cottages. Adjoining was a private house, where Messrs. Gilliam and Son's statuary showrooms and residence now stand. Messrs. Butcher and Son's confectioner's shop had for owner and occupier Mr. Thomas Rose. The next house was occupied by his son, Mr. Thos. Rose, jun. He was a grocer and pork butcher, and did very well for some years. After the death of his wife he emigrated to Australia. The old carrier previously mentioned lived in the next house. "The King's Arms," kept by Mrs. Mills, came next, and between it and the open space, now the site of the butcher's shop, was a little room used as a cobbler's stall. An old man named Slipper had it. His son emigrated to America, and did wonderfully well there. After old Slipper a little old man named Robinson had it. He was very greatly respected by all who knew him. Where the butcher's shop now stands there was an open space(2) with grass in the middle and shrubs at the sides. A road was afterwards made down it for the use of the brewery.

(1) 1912 Girl's High School; 1952 H.G. Kingham's offices; 1977 W.H. Cullen's offices.
(2) 1912 butcher's shop; 1977 Dorking Floors.

Attlee's Reminiscences of Old Dorking

Dorking Changes

Vanished or Vanishing Industries

Seventy years ago Dorking was a busy little town, and many thriving businesses were carried on in it and in its vicinity. There were the various corn mills on the Pippbrook, the first of which was the Rookery Mill, carried on by Mr. Joshua Rose; then the Westcott Mill, where Mr. James Bravery did a considerable trade. Next on the stream was Milton Court Mill, which, with the Milton Court Farm, was occupied by Mr. John Wells. Coming into the town itself, there was the Parsonage Mill, carried on by Mr. Richard Attlee, whose grandson, Mr. Edmund W. Attlee, now uses it. The Pippbrook Mill was owned and occupied by Mr. John Abel, and the Pixham Mill had for owner and occupier Mr. James Dewdney. The Castle Mill on the river Mole was used by Mr. George Dewdney. All these mills did a fair trade and gave employment to a number of hands. The Rookery Mill, Westcott Mill and Milton Court Mill are now unoccupied and are shut up. Formerly there was a windmill on the Holmwood, and the miller, Mr. Hutchins, did a good business there.

Then there were the maltings. Mr. Cheesman had a malthouse at Milton, and Mr. Young, Mr. Lucock, Mr. Richard Attlee, and Mr. Boxall had one each in the town, all of which provided employment. Not one of them is now in use. Mr. Batchelor had one at Betchworth, which is also unoccupied.

Formerly Mr. James Cheesman had a brewery in South-street, Mr. Young one in Church-street, and Mrs. Hay, Mr. Lucock and Mr. Boxall one each in High-street. These are all closed, and there is no beer brewed in Dorking now, not even in private houses.

Mr. Samuel Bothwell had the lime works and did a very large business. He sent enormous quantities of lime to the suburbs of London, which were just then beginning to be developed.

Attlee's Reminiscences of Old Dorking

Mr. Young, Mr. Fuller, Mr. Bowring and others had brick yards, where vast numbers of bricks were made, and met with a ready sale.

Two coopers and two basketmakers plied their several trades, and got a living; now there is not one of either calling in the place.

In 1837 Mr. Robert Best Ede was appointed chemist to the young Queen; he did a very large business in perfumery and toilet requisites, which he supplied wholesale to many London firms. He also had the Post Office and printing works, employing many hands. He died in 1845, and the business was sold to a firm, who failed to carry it on successfully.

There were two candle factories in Dorking, and one at Mickleham; all three were thriving businesses then, but are now extinct.

There was formerly a pottery, just opposite where the North Holmwood Church now stands. Flower pots and other coarse ware were made there, but it never seems to have been a very profitable business.

There was a rope maker at Flint Hill, who did a fair business and brought his goods into the market every Thursday afternoon.

There was a fowl market every Thursday in the forenoon. A great many farmers brought in fat fowls in crates; these fetched high prices, and were eagerly bought up by higglers for the London trade. The fowls were all of the old-fashioned large dark Dorking breed, which when crammed sold well. In the spring from seven to eight shillings each was a common price for them, and at Christmas fifteen shillings each was readily given for fat capons. From the "Bull's Head" Inn to where the London, County and Westminster Bank now stands, the pavement was studded with crates of fowls, and crowded with the farmers' wives, who sold the birds after they had themselves crammed them. Now no fowls are brought in for sale, and no farmers' wives cram them.

Attlee's Reminiscences of Old Dorking

Seventy years ago it was very difficult to buy a single fowl for the table. All those brought in on Thursday were cleared out of the town by four o'clock in the afternoon. Some of the townspeople used to buy a few runners, as they were called, and fat them for themselves, in coops, without cramming them. There were no regular poulterers' shops in Dorking then. Sometimes the landlord of the "Bull's Head" (Mr. Joseph Woodroffe) was able to supply dead poultry, but the price was too high for most people.

Attlee's Reminiscences of Old Dorking

Queen Victoria's Jubilee, 1887

The news columns of the Dorking Advertiser of June 25th, 1887, were devoted to a report of the local celebration of Queen Victoria's Jubilee, to the total exclusion of every other news item, from which we may draw the conclusion that the appetite of the newspaper reader of those days was not so satiable as it is now.

Dorking, we read, celebrated the event "right loyally, joyfully and successfully..... Never in the history of our little town did it present a scene so brilliant, so gay and so festive, as the rays of sunshine shone upon the bright colours of the banners, bannerettes and flags, which over-arched the streets and hung from almost every window, lattice and available projecture, making them appear, ever and anon as they were lashed in the wind, like flashes of light almost dazzling in their brilliancy. At night, when the great Illuminator had sunk beneath the horizon, the scene changed from one of bright festive gayness to that of a gorgeous carnival-like splendour. Myriads of jets arranged in pleasing devices and of every possible colour illuminated the streets throughout the whole town."

After this pretty word picture perhaps a brief reference to the day's programme may not be without interest. At 9.15 there was a church parade of the various public bodies and societies, including the Rifle Volunteers, under the command of Capt. Young, the Oddfellows and Foresters, the Town Brass and Drum and Fife Bands, the Fire Brigade, Young Men's Friendly Society, the Ambulance Corps, and the Good Templars, the whole being marshalled by Capt. Shearburn. The church was crowded, and the address was given by the Vicar, the Rev. E.A. Chichester. At noon a grand procession was formed on Spittal Heath, and in addition to the foregoing included the elementary school children, the Rev. H.C. Sturdy being in charge of those of St. Paul's, the Rev. G. Avery the British,

Attlee's Reminiscences of Old Dorking

and the Rev. Father Volckeryck the Roman Catholic. "The procession now moves on en route for the Nower, via High-street, South-street, Horsham-road and Knoll-road. A large crowd gather in the streets; either side of the streets are thronged with hundreds of spectators, and upper windows and balconies are crowded. Nay, the very housetops are made grand stands pro tem. For, look up South-street, and you see several persons on the top of a house there, and among them is a young lady trepidly standing unsupported, the wind ruffling her attire as it did that of Pope Sappho as she views the sea from a prominent rock." Arriving at the Nower nearly a thousand people were provided at 2.30 with dinner, served by Mr. Graves (Red Lion Hotel), and laid out on 16 tables fully 50 yards in length. "The tables are under the presidency of Messrs. Butler, Gilliam, Mason, Marsh, Mathews" - and then follow the bracketed words, "You say more to come?" apparently an aside between the printer and the scribe which most unfortunately miscarried. Liquid refreshments, the report goes on to state are served in "jam pots, brown jugs, tea cups, basins and tea cans," and the guests brought with them every kind of cutlery, "except scissors and scythes." At the close of the repast, and Mr. Durrant having thanked the army of waiters who by reason of their numbers and the restricted space evidently had a real lively time of it, the I.C.U. Minstrels gave an entertainment, but as the wind blew in the wrong direction, the stage arrangements being faulty, "not more than a dozen or two could see the darkies or could hear them." Among the individual performers were Messrs. G. Smith, W. Ison, Greathurst, J. Walker, Whaley, D. Combe, W. Verner and A. Letts. Sports commenced at 4 o'clock, and among the successful competitors we notice Sydney Fuller (who won the high jump), Bacon, "Duckey" Rose, H. West, Hudson, Bristow, F. Balchin, T. Jones, Peters, Miller (hurdle race), Burrell, Curtain, T. Lee, Chitty, Marsden and Rose (three-legged race),

Attlee's Reminiscences of Old Dorking

F. Hudson (sack and wheelbarrow races); and in the girls' races Agnes Shearman, Laura Strudwick and Edith Curn. The tug-of-war was won by Messrs. Stone and Turner's employees. Mrs. Chichester gave away the prizes, and thanks were afterwards passed to her, as well as to Mr. Durrant (chairman of the Jubilee Committee), and to Mr. H. Chaldecott (hon. secretary). A bonfire, 30 ft. high and 120 ft. round its base, and built under the superintendence of Mr. G.S. Mathews, was lighted by Mr. R. Barclay at 10.20, at which time 17 other fires could be counted on the neighbouring hills. Half an hour later the masqueraders who were to form the torchlight procession were marshalled. The commander-in-chief was Mr. E. Miles, whose staff included Messrs. G. Shearburn, T.G. Rix, A. Letts, H.E. Miller, Adsett, J.A. White, W.S. Fuller and H. Adams. The Captain of Fire was Mr. W. Stone, and Lieutenant, Mr. H.E. Turner; Captain of Torches, Mr. A.G. Brandram, Lieutenant, Mr. H. Butler; Captain of Band, Mr. Sherlock, Lieutenant, Mr. G.E.P. Butt. After the town had been paraded two bonfires made of the torches were lighted in front of the Red Lion Hotel, and just as the Parish Church bells struck the midnight hour "a thousand voices of the people who surrounded the burning torches sang out right heartily and lustily 'God Save the Queen.' Thus ended, in Dorking, the day memorable in the history of the town, in the history of the country, and in the history of the world."

RECOLLECTIONS OF OLD DORKING

by
William Dinnage

KOHLER AND COOMBES
DORKING
1977

Dinnage's Recollections of Old Dorking

William Henry Dinnage

Born January 1870, son of Henry & Rana Dinnage of 7 Hampstead Road, Dorking. Died February 1963.

In 1950, soon after his retirement, William Dinnage began to put on paper recollections of his early life. Partly revised in 1960, his writings were published in the Dorking Advertiser during the summer of 1963, a few months after his death. He wrote mainly of his boyhood days during the 1870s and early 1880s.

His long working life was spent with the Dorking timber firm, Brooker's. Starting as a very young clerk, he became the mainstay of the firm's office, his copperplate handwriting a memento of a bygone standard of excellence.

In 1900 he married Mary Sarah Williams, whose widowed mother occupied the caretaker's cottage at the Friends Meeting House on Butter Hill. Moving in, William Dinnage and his wife began fifty years of caring for the building and for all who used it.

When almost eighty he retired to Woodgate in South Terrace, and it was from there that he took the walks around Tower Hill and down into the south end of the town which he had known so well as a boy.

A quiet unassuming man, a great reader and a gifted draughtsman, he was a most rewarding companion to all who had his confidence. Walking with him one day, a newcomer to Dorking observed how William Dinnage was nodding 'Good-day' all along the High Street. "Why, Mr. Dinnage, you must know almost everyone in Dorking!" "Yes," he replied, "of a certain class - I believe I do."

The last few years of his long life he spent happily in Worthing.

Dinnage's Recollections of Old Dorking

Southern end of Dorking

I propose to walk in imagination through the streets of Dorking, and recall the places and people, and note the changes that have taken place since the earliest days of my life.

I will start from the southern end of the town, from what is now called South-terrace, where there stood a large house, faced with flint, known as Woodhurst. This was empty for many months before it was demolished in 1959, and with its surrounding grounds became what is now 1 to 6 Woodhurst.

The large house referred to was inhabited by two old maiden ladies named Squire, who were members of the Society of Friends. The houses opposite, on the north side, were built in the 1930s on land which formed the kitchen garden of Woodhurst.

This land joined the estate of Denfield, the site of a mansion occupied by the Misses Flood, and at their death by a nephew with family, who, when Tower Hill became less select, sold the estate to be developed by speculative builders. Speaking of the Flood family, I may mention that a brother, who lived also at Denfield with his sisters at an earlier date was a curate at Dorking Parish Church.

Speaking of the parish church I well remember a popular curate by the name of the Rev. Geoffrey Hughes. I met him often, when a little chap on my way to Sunday School, in the Horsham-road on his way to the Union Workhouse to minister to the inmates.

The Rev. Neville G. Stiff, in his book on the St. Martin's Church, says that on the resignation of Mr. Hughes from St. Martin's to an appointment at Woolston, Southampton, he received as a testimonial a cheque for £300.

Leaving South-terrace and walking down the slope we come to Harrow-road East. The houses on the left side had very hilly gardens down to the road. I remember, as a boy, watching the building. I had a schoolmate whose family moved into the first built,

Dinnage's Recollections of Old Dorking

from Harrow Gate-gardens.

Next is now known as Priory Bungalow, site of the Dorking water works, the pumping engine being housed and working here, together with the engineer's quarters. The engineer's name was Collins. The tall chimney from the furnace that heated the boiler of the engine belched out a cloud of black smoke and the chimney had a deep iron grating at the top.

We now come to a road on the left - an incline up to Tower Hill, and Bentworth Priors (keeping left). The largish houses at the back of the old water works site, Clovelly and Woodlands, were not then in existence.

Walking up the inclined road we come to three houses on the right, one of which, in my early days was occupied by Sir Arthur and Lady Cotton and their daughter. She was afterwards Lady Hope, who married Admiral Sir James Hope of Carriden, Nr. Linlithgow and Bo'ness, Scotland. Sir Arthur Cotton, did much useful work at irrigation in India, and was known as Irrigation Cotton. His detractors said he had water on the brain.

I remember seeing the carriages of Lady Hope's wedding go along the main Horsham-road on their way to St. Paul's Church, where she was married. Sir Arthur used to ride a tricycle, which was then a newly-introduced means of transport for elderly men which came about the same period as the penny-farthing bicycle.

The tricycle had more than one design in those days, and one consisted of a large wheel on one side, and small wheels opposite and back, the rider sitting in the centre of the machine and guiding by a kind of stirrup handle nearly on a level with the rider's seat. This was the kind Sir Arthur rode.

Sir Arthur Cotton left the house mentioned in late 1870s and had a house built in what is now Tower Hill-road, which he named Woodcote after his native village in Oxfordshire. This he occupied for many years.

Dinnage's Recollections of Old Dorking

It is, at the time of writing these recollections, known as "The Garth" Nursing Home. In Sir Arthur's day there was no entrance to the house and grounds from the main Horsham turn-pike, but the entrance and high walls were built by a Mr. Hubbard, a previous owner of Woodcote before it became a nursing home.

Sir Arthur was very popular as a supporter of evangelical and temperance work in Dorking. As I am recalling people, as well as places, I must mention the enthusiastic activities of his daughter Miss Cotton, afterwards Lady Hope, who then shared her father's zeal for the spread of the gospel temperance message in the district.

Miss Cotton held simple religious meetings in what were then known as "The Beckenham Rooms" behind, and I think owned by Mr. Job Pledge, who had his building yard at the southern end of Falkland-road.

Mr. (or Old Job) Pledge, was a large-hearted, kindly man, and it was these rooms that he allowed the Salvation Army, then extremely unpopular, to use as a barracks on their first 'invasion' of Dorking - many years after Miss Cotton's activities. She wrote two books on the mission she started, particularly among the men, which also included a coffee room at Beckenham Rooms, with a coffee barrow, which was used to convey hot coffee and other beverages to the rougher working men who began work at about 6 o'clock in the morning.

The estate now known as Cliftonville and the new roads cut on the Harrowgate estates - Knoll-road, Roman-road, and Ridgeway-road - were then requiring an extra number of men to be employed and work in the district as navvies and bricklayers and labourers, so a cup of hot coffee was very welcome, and soon found eager consumers.

It kept the men from drinking cold beer, which they did not hesitate to do even on the coldest mornings. I have seen three teams of horses and three timber carriages outside a beershop, for twenty minutes at a time, while the

Dinnage's Recollections of Old Dorking

carters were inside drinking cold beer on a cold, frosty morning near 7 o'clock.

Miss Cotton held gospel meetings in these rooms (as well as running a coffee room) on certain week-nights, and always on Sunday afternoons, and I well remember on several occasions being taken there by my father and noticing the few coloured prints on the walls - "The Good Shepherd" and other similar scenes from the gospels. And also I have a recollection of a kind of meeting room smell, which was always keenly perceptible to my young boyish nostrils. This I think was caused by the men's clothes, for the attenders were men well steeped in the smoke from their clay pipes, and soaked in perspiration to saturation point, especially in summer time, the season of my visits.

This was the time when the revival power generated in the religious world by the great missions conducted by the evangelists Moody and Sankey was in full force, and they were on their visits to England from U.S.A. in the '70s. The hymns sung at the Beckenham Rooms were those used at the great evangelist's missions sung and compiled by Ira D. Sankey, and Miss Cotton taught these hymns, playing a small harmonium, or what was I think called a flutina, on her lap.

It was at one of these meetings that I first heard sung "There were Ninety and Nine", the song that Sankey sang with so much feeling to the multitudes who flocked to huge meetings of the mission in the large towns.

While trying to tell of this lady's work, I will mention what was done nearer the centre of the town. A coffee room was started in one of the lower rooms of the public hall (now the Fire Station) in West-street: the room on the right, looking at the building from West-street, and immediately next to Mr. Woodland's stone yard. This room is, or was afterwards, used by the ambulance authorities.

Miss Cotton also conducted a Sunday evening service at 8.0 o'clock, in the large upper room at the public hall. Although this was

Dinnage's Recollections of Old Dorking

timed to begin after the churches of the town had closed their doors on Sundays, a good number of the congregation of Miss Cotton were non-church-goers. These services drew large audiences, and Miss Cotton became popular. She had a pleasing, engaging manner, and silvery voice, and her message was simple, and suited to the way-faring men and women who listened.

They were addresses in which anecdote was aptly interspersed, and they had a strong emotional appeal. The hymns sung were from the new Moody and Sankey selection, which were becoming popular.

These "Sacred Songs and Solos" were published by Messrs. Morgan & Scott, of whom the partner Mr. Robert Scott lived at Ribblesdale, Horsham-road, Dorking.

One could often hear these and others of equal popularity hummed or whistled by boys and people in the daily walks of life.

Mr. Brace, a missioner, was engaged to carry on with the work which had become an organised and popular institution, and a Mr. Gooding to work the coffee room.

It is not surprising that with money and live enthusiasm for mission work having got so popular and established the promoters should want it to expand and find premises that could be called their own. So a hall was built of corrugated galvanised iron in what is now Junction-road, and West-street, with accommodation for the resident Missioner (Brace) and the manager of the coffee room.

The coffee room was built with its frontage in West-street, and was very much in appearance as at the time of writing these notes in 1959-60. It had kitchens and stores, and offices necessary for its maintenance at the back in Junction-road, and a passage way in, to the left of the lecture hall and the buildings of the coffee room on the right.

On the corner of Junction-road Mr. Grinstead had his building business, later taken over by Mr. Cole and, on his death, by Mr. John Fell.

Dinnage's Recollections of Old Dorking

I remember a lively fortnight's mission being held, when Wm. Noble, the founder of the Blue Ribbon Army, came with his vim and humour. What a rousing time it was! Mr. Noble was an entertaining speaker, his addresses full of humour and anecdote and his delivery full of action, and withal of Gospel flavour, and having the power of arousing the emotions of his audience by their unfailing method of introducing gospel choruses, which were sung with much gusto by the crowded congregation.

Mr. Noble had a good English concertina of which he was an expert exponent, and would entertain his audiences during the course of his meetings. The central home of this temperance movement was then at Hoxton Hall, and was largely supported by the Society of Friends (Quakers) Wm. Isaac Palmer, of Reading, having purchased the hall, an old music hall in Hoxton. Mr. Noble was a staunch Quaker and on a visit to New York (where he met John B. Gough, a great temperance convert and orator) he received his chief inspiration for his gospel temperance work which he started in East London.

So it came to pass that on one or two occasions during the campaign at Dorking lecture hall, Wm. Noble brought a very fine gifted tenor singer - who was a helper and worker in the growing mission at Hoxton - to delight the crowded hall at Dorking with his singing. The name of this gifted singer was Mr. J. Ogram Webb, who after a time succeeded Mr. Brace as the Missioner of the lecture hall, and whose singing and work for many years made a lasting impression on the people of Dorking, and whose memory will be fragrant for many years to come.

Mr. Webb got a very efficient choir together, which was accompanied by a large American organ, played in later days of the mission by Miss N. Todman, and one of his most popular attractions to the hall was a weekly evening for the people. Mr. Webb had been a fairly wide traveller, both over the British Isles and on the Continent of Europe, and was in possession of a large number of views,

Dinnage's Recollections of Old Dorking

which he had taken and made into lantern slides. So he was able to give his lectures by the aid of his magic lantern. These evenings proved very attractive, and became well attended.

This was all before the cinema became the centre of entertainment. Admission was free and these talks were pervaded with the Christian spirit and the savour of the gospel message. Another much favoured institution was the activity of the Band of Hope, a junior temperance movement, which drew a large number of young people into its ranks in those days. It was a movement that extended all over the Kingdom. The Lecture Hall Band of Hope was not the first in Dorking, for a large one was established at the Congregational Church some years earlier.

When Miss Cotton had become Lady Hope the time came when she removed from Dorking to join Sir James in Scotland, where he had supported a mission at Carriden, Bo'ness, on the Firth of Forth. This mission included a coffee room, and a Dorking man and his wife were invited to help in the management of it. There was also a bath connected, and many rough sailors and men who brought loads of pit props from Scandinavia to Bo'ness in those days were catered for, and brought under the influence of the gospel temperance message. Unfortunately these rooms had been built on land over coal mines, and eventually, because the foundations gave way, they had to be abandoned.

When rumours of the probable departure of Lady Hope from Dorking got abroad, a large number of people were greatly disturbed, and when she left the town her helpers and followers, which at the time included a good number of working men, formed the bulk of the congregations at the lecture hall, about to be built. Mr. Denny, who later was to become the second husband of Lady Hope and who had a large house at the foot of Box Hill, gave liberally to the support of the mission and to a large extent took it into his charge. One working man I know wrote a number of verses voicing the sorrow of his

Dinnage's Recollections of Old Dorking

fellows at the departure of Lady Hope from among them.

Mr. Brace, the first superintending missioner, left to take up work with Mr. Fegan's homes for boys. He was engaged, when I last heard of him, in charge of the boys who were found a place in the U.S.A. and Canada, seeing them safely across to the New World, establishing their future in their fresh spheres of life.

As already stated Mr. J. Ogram Webb was then offered, and accepted, the charge of the missioner of the lecture hall.

After this long digression, I come back to the road on Tower Hill where Sir Arthur Cotton first lived, and continue on towards the Tower itself. We take the road to the left towards Bentworth Priors.

The occupant in my young days was Callen, and subsequently a Mr. Hall, who gave a bandstand to the town when the widening of South-street took place. Now the bandstand has been replaced by an ornamental garden. The land between Bentworth Priors and the next, going up the incline, was all vacant until the 1950s. The next house was the one annexed to the tower itself. I remember going to the foot of the tower on one occasion, probably when the house was empty, and seeing a date cut in a stone low down on the tower. It was 1829.

I have an old view showing Dorking at the time of the first Parish Church, looking across the town from the old lime works to Tower Hill, and the only building shown on this eminence is the tower itself, and quite bare of trees. I knew four of the occupiers of the house annexed to the tower - one a Mr. Keel who my father supplied with footwear, and I, as a boy, had to walk up to the house to deliver boots.

Another gentleman who lived at the Tower House was a Mr. Davis, whose son had a large astronomical telescope fitted in one of the rooms. I belonged at that time to a Young Men's Society. I think in connection with

Dinnage's Recollections of Old Dorking

St. Paul's Church, of which young Mr. Davis was also a member. One of our fellow-members gave a paper on astronomy, or it may have been "The Moon", and Mr. Davis, being present, offered one or two members especially interested up to his house to view the moon through his telescope.

I jumped at the opportunity, and with a like-minded mate, went up to Tower House on a clear night when the moon was about half full. The telescope was one that was caused to keep pace with the earth's diurnal motion by a clockwork arrangement, and so keeping pace with the moon which would otherwise soon be out of the ken of the object glass.

I have never forgotten the view of the moon I had in Tower House, where I saw the familiar ruler of the night in reality in close detail, with the high parts of its surface catching the sunlight as dots of light in advance, before the bulk of the body rotated into the full sunshine.

The next occupant of Tower House I knew was the Rev. G.K. Olivier, who came from Guildford School to Dorking to open the school on Tower Hill, and later gave up the school to become a curate at St. Martin's Church. He played both football and cricket for the town teams. His son, now Sir Laurence Olivier, was born at 26 Wathen-road during the time his father was curate at Dorking.

Still proceeding up the road we pass a few yards on the left hand side, opposite the tower, a large house, which is called Oakhurst, which was with the exception of Goodwyns, the last large house built on the hill. Oakhurst occupies land that I can remember being thinnish woodland, and containing four or five large trees, one of which I managed to climb as a boy. On the same side of the road (left) down a rough track was the reservoir, which I remember going down into on one occasion when it was under repair, with a mate whose father was working as a bricklayer at the repairing job.

Now, following along the road which bears to

Dinnage's Recollections of Old Dorking

the right, we note a house on the right hand side named Thirlestane where lived at one time an artist by the name of Biscombe-Gardiner, and from the front of the house looking west, one could see the Church of St. Martha at Chilworth. After passing this house on the right a short distance further on we come to a large house on the left hand side quite close to the road. This house could be seen on the skyline from the Horsham turnpike road if one looked up to the wooded eminence.

This house was of dark coloured tile facing, and I think was called Oakridge. I recall the occupants of this house as the Down family, Mr. Dondas Down being a solicitor having his offices in High Street, and still carried on in the name of Down, Scott & Down.

Mr. Scott joined the firm of lawyers when old Mr. Down's son was also in the business and lived in the Harrow-road West, at the end house on the right. I remember seeing old Mr. Down often, with tall hat and dark clothes, walking along the high path in Horsham-road of an evening, going home from his office in the town. He was of middle height, clean-shaven, slightly ruddy cheeks, and rather pleasing countenance. Two of his sons, William and Frank, were in the business at a later date to that of which I am writing which would be about 1879/80. One son (W.J.) built Elmhurst in the lower part of the Tower Hill-road, and opposite what was Woodcote.

I do not know any exact details of what happened after the decease of old Mr. and Mrs. Down, but I do know that the property came eventually into the hands of a Mr. Powell, who proved afterwards to be a great benefactor to the old British School, making it possible to build the school in what is now Norfolk-road, and known as the Powell Corderoy School.

I used to see Mr. Powell often driving down the Vincents-road in a largish Governess trap, on his way to the Dorking S.E. & C. Rly. Station, where he took train daily for London. However, Mr. Powell pulled down the

Dinnage's Recollections of Old Dorking

old house next to the road, and rebuilt it, but chose a site farther back, and somewhat higher than the road and of the old house, and so obtained a fine view to the south, of Holmwood Common and Redland Woods. This new house was larger than the old one along the roadside, and I am not sure if he named it Oakridge, but it was in after years, when acquired by Mr. Martineau, known as Goodwyns. There was a farm below the eminence on which the new house stood and still stands, called Goodwyns Farm, which I well remember.

The farmhouse was old, rather tall, and stood on grassland well away from the public road at Flint Hill. A rough hedge bounded the farmland from the road, starting at the old cottage on left going south, opposite the "Windmill Inn" (where there was a wide grass verge on which was a rope walk) and extending to a short distance of the Bents Brook where it was very swampy on the right hand side of the turnpike.

There was a field gate into the Goodwyns farm land at this end on the left. This farm was occupied by two men known to me, the first by old Wm. Jeal, who had a business in Falkland-road, and of whom a reference later, and the second a Mr. Fairbrother, son of the proprietor of the "Windmill Inn".

In a book written by Mr. Cousin, a former headmaster of the old British School, at the time it was removed from Church-street and the new one built in Norfolk-road, it is stated that Mr. Powell died suddenly of a seizure on Jan. 15, 1901. But I have a recollection that his death was caused by a tragic happening to him at the building of his new house at Tower Hill. At the time it was reported that he slipped from part of the scaffolding when inspecting progress of the work and this fall may have resulted in the seizure referred to. However, his loss to the cause of undenominational education was greatly mourned, and the school is a lasting memorial to his great generosity. Miss Corderoy the other indefatigable worker for the building of the school lived with Miss Marshall on Cliftonville, and afterwards

Dinnage's Recollections of Old Dorking

built a house near the junction of Knoll and Roman-road, known as "Rooftree".

Leaving now the scene of these events and the disappearance of old houses, and the building of new, we proceed down this top road which is enclosed in woodland and copse, as the houses to the left on the bend were not built when I knew the road when a boy. The road takes a sharp turn to the right and leads us to a spot where we took the road a short time ago which leads to Bentworth Priors.

A few yards again, and we arrive back at the houses before mentioned which was the first home of Sir Arthur Cotton in Dorking. I should here mention that I am not sure at the time of recording these recollections in which of the two houses standing in this road Sir Arthur lived; whether the one standing at the time of writing, or the one that has long disappeared. They were side by side. The one that has not survived to the present day was farthest from the top of the steps, leading down to the Harrow-road East down which we will go. The house that has disappeared was similar to the one now standing and occupied and was a long time empty and gradually became very dilapidated, and was finally demolished. The house had the reputation for a long time of being haunted.

Now descending the steps we come into the Harrow-road East which road we left earlier on. The cottages on the right hand side were built before my time. Proceeding down the hill we note a largish house, the second one on the right hand, which was occupied by the Bargman family. Mr. Bargman started a painter's and decorator's business at the top of Junction-road, a branch of a London business.

Next to his house in the Harrow-road was a very old cottage, which I imagine to have been 300 years old, and perhaps the only dwelling (with its next door neighbour at the corner of Horsham turnpike) a century ago, on the whole of the hill, when it was more bare of trees and comparatively open.

When I was a small boy, a man by the name of

Dinnage's Recollections of Old Dorking

Dearling lived at this old cottage. He was a chimney sweep, and I used to go there to order the old man to come and sweep the chimney - a tall one - of our house. For his services my mother paid his charge, usually 6d. at that time, and no tip!

The large house opposite on left hand side called then, as now, Harrow Lodge, was occupied by Mr. Butler. He was a grocer and had a licence to sell intoxicants, and his shop was in South-street opposite The Rotunda, where he kept his stores. Mr. Butler was a man just above medium height, with a sunny brown moustache and moderate beard, and a benign face.

He was a man with great appreciation of music, himself an accomplished musician having a small church organ in his house. He had sons and two daughters, the elder of which was engaged to a curate of St. Paul's. But owing to some disclosures he had made of his life in the past, which came to her knowledge, no marriage resulted from the engagement.

Mr. Butler also had a branch shop at the corner of Falkland-road and Barrington-road, opposite the Falkland Arms, and his manager there was a Mr. Stitson. When Mr. Stitson left Mr. Butler appointed Mr. Plant, whose family I knew very well, to succeed him.

After a while Mr. Plant, Senior, acquired the shop and started business on his own account. He greatly enlarged the scope of the business, and dealt in such articles as sewing machines, mangles, and perhaps bicycles and crockenware, all in addition to the grocery and provision business, and was very successful.

Coming back to Harrow-road East, the next plot after Harrow Lodge was a small market garden which extended to the main road turnpike and was tended by a man named Alec Robinson. Houses now stand on this plot. Now we will cross the turnpike and go up the incline of Harrow-road West.

This road should be particularly interesting and familiar to me, as it was my first playground as a very little boy, when I could

Dinnage's Recollections of Old Dorking

safely be allowed out of our garden gate on my own.

Harrow-road West was at the top of our longish garden and three or four of the top garden gates, whose frontages are in the Hampstead-road, opened into it, including ours. Harrow-road West, at the part outside our gate, was very rough at that time, with wide irregular verges of couch grass, dandelions and other weeds growing in healthy splendour and matching the big loose stones and brickbats and water channels that graced the surface of the road for a considerable distance.

The traffic at this time was practically nil, such as there was being an occasional tradesman's cart moving at walking pace. So here we could play in comfort, within sight of Tower Hill and the fields which are now Cliftonville, and the Glory Woods.

We played games with a ball, which often went over into a neighbours' garden. One neighbour - at Rose Cottage which is still in existence - at length got very angry with us and threatened to withhold the ball on many occasions. She was an irascible woman who lived with a man who was extremely fat and who spent a large portion of his spring and summer time bending over the fence from the outside, smoking his pipe and looking towards the house and garden.

I think he was too stout to walk far. He died, though, and when the funeral had to take place, his coffin was too big to get out of the house excepting through his bedroom window, which to my young mind, as I witnessed the novel operation, was a proceeding which was of the utmost dismay and fear lest they allowed the coffin to drop on to the garden below.

Opposite our garden gate and hedges was a high brick wall, which enclosed land which I think was the kitchen garden of the people in the house below, Edgecombe, on the Horsham turn-pike. It was occupied then by a Mr. Thorn. This land was later used by the brothers Len and Fred Pledge.

Dinnage's Recollections of Old Dorking

Some distance farther over on this land was in my early days a large tall elm tree, which could be seen well in its stateliness from the back bedroom window of our house. There was a path each side of the Harrowroad West. That on the opposite side was a little raised from the road level, with a small grass verge.

A few paces farther up the hill on the right we come to a large villa Fernside, where lived at the time about which I am writing two sister maiden ladies, the Misses Cooper. One was rather tall, and the other very short. Both were district visitors in connection with St. Paul's Church, and also collected from the poorer of the parishioners where we lived weekly payments for clubs to enable them to purchase coal and clothing on more easy terms at Christmas.

The tall Miss Cooper collected for the coal, and the little Miss Cooper for the clothing. The latter loaned, for the edification and improvement of the minds of the parishioners of her district, a weekly copy of the "Sunday at Home" (now extinct), usually out of date and not consecutive, so any continuous tale in the magazine could not be followed. I as a little boy, being able to read fairly for my years, read some of the contents.

The same lady also brought along a toy at Christmas. I think my brothers were then but small babies and I was the recipient, so I looked upon her with more friendly eyes than the tall Miss Cooper, whom I thought more abrupt, and tended to retire without wasting much time in conversation.

The two Miss Coopers did not as a rule visit at the same time. A card was supplied to the parishioner who paid in her money to these ladies, on which they recorded the weekly payments. I was often present in our front room when these ladies called and noticed with what care the small Miss Cooper would record the amount paid and go over it several times, with her thin lead pencil, to make it quite indelible and almost impossible to remove without leaving a deep impression. By

Dinnage's Recollections of Old Dorking

this means she avoided the unlikely possibility of any alteration by a miscreant member of the parish who might have the satanic urge to make a 6d. into a 1s., and so confuse the club's accounts when paying out time came.

When I was a little older the ladies, regarding our family as quite exemplary and worthy of encouragement - and I suppose me a willing and honest boy - asked me to come to their house to scoop out the daisy roots from their lawn. I had to do so without making any big holes, inroads into the lawn, or causing any disfigurement. I was provided with a trug basket to convey the daisy roots to a rubbish heap under the strict surveillance of the tall Miss Cooper. The remuneration they thought to make to me was, to my boyish mind rather trifling; but no doubt in their view it was quite adequate to the services rendered. When my mates were playing in the road outside on a summer evening my possessive faculty was greatly lessened, and I am afraid had the effect of a diminishing attendance at the Misses Coopers and causing the daisies to become more conspicuous upon their lawn, so they had to employ a little pressure on me to "do" the daisies, as they termed my employment!

When quite young I had the measles and was kept abed in my room looking on this house, and I well remember how a flock of swifts used to fly loudly squealing round and round one of the chimney stacks. I have not seen any of these birds for many years, but our insect pests have been on the increase!

The Misses Cooper left this house some years after these happenings, and went to The Falklands, a house nearer the Coldharbour-road end of Harrow-road West.

Now a glance at the opposite side of the road. After the garden with the high brick wall mentioned came a largish house where lived for a time a Mr. Martin who was a solicitor in the then firm of Hart & Martin - now Hart, Scales & Hodges.

After this house was a large garden, entered by a gate, with tall quickset hedges at each

Dinnage's Recollections of Old Dorking

side, tended and cultivated by a Mr. Stringer, of Vincent-road. After he gave up it was taken over by Mr. Arthur Chalcraft, who employed his brother Billy to work in it.

I remember Mr. Arthur Chalcraft at the time he started his business in a very humble way, going round with potatoes for sale on a wheelbarrow. Being a go-ahead man he worked up a very considerable florist and nursery business. He acquired a long greenhouse in South-street, which was previously worked by a Mr. Harry Lucas, opposite what is now May's garage and show rooms. Afterwards he started working land at the Punch Bowl, Reigate-road, with sons in the business.

As a young man, Mr. Arthur Chalcraft was an early cyclist. As a small boy, I saw him trying to ride an old wooden boneshaker - as those early bicycles were called - and afterwards when the pennyfarthing type were invented, riding one of these. However, being an exceptionally short man, and although he had a low machine, he could not reach the pedals and so had to fix wooden blocks on them to enable him to propel the bicycle.

He did not, I think even when the "Safety" became the standard type, ever become a cyclist in after years. His early efforts did not have the effect of making him feel too safe or comfortable in the saddle.

Going back to his garden in Harrow-road West, and proceeding up the hill, the next large houses were "Upland Villas", a semi-detached pair, where lived Miss Utterton, who I think was sister to Canon Utterton, sometime rector or vicar of Leatherhead.

In the other lived the Misses White, sisters of the founders of the estate agency firm of White & Sons in the High-street. One of these ladies lived to be a hundred, and a former Congregational Minister, the Rev. Tom R. Grantham, said in my hearing that he intended to call on the lady to present his congratulations so that he could say he had shaken hands with a centenarian. People who lived to a hundred years were rare in my earlier days.

Dinnage's Recollections of Old Dorking

Upland Villas commanded a pleasant view towards the hills at Denbies, and immediately in front of these houses on the opposite side of the road is the Bunkers Hill - now called Falkland Hill, but known in my young days by the former name - which at this point joined the Harrow-road West. The hill was in line with Falkland-road.

I am always interested in the origins of the names of roads and streets, and a few in Dorking are known to me, but I have never heard why this hill was known as Bunkers Hill. The guess I have made is that it may have been made or cut at the time of the American War of Independence when the Battle of Bunkers Hill was fought in 1775.

On the right hand side going down the hill, there was a large block of ugly flint-faced houses where a poor class of people lived, making a contrast to the more peaceful Harrow-road West. These houses were entered from the path of the road by a passage in which were the doors to each house.

When Leslie-road and Moleside at Pixham were developed, a number of these poorer people migrated, to make their home in the Pixham locality.

I was once told by an older resident of the Hampstead-road who, I knew very well, that there was a time when it was proposed that Dorking should be made into a military town after the style of Aldershot. Dorking was then surrounded by the estates of three large land-owners, who not because they objected to war, but because they strongly objected to having the pleasant and attractive little town with its surrounding beautiful scenery marred by barracks and soldiers around the district put their spokes in the wheel. By their strong influence and objections the scheme did not materialise.

I mention this because these ugly houses at Bunkers Hill were said to have been built in anticipation of using them for possible barracks. This hill was in my early days very rough, with plenty of large stones and brickbats on the surface. No doubt the

Dinnage's Recollections of Old Dorking

water from heavy rains that rushed down the hill washed away the smaller gravel.

At the top of the hill and partly in Harrow-road West, there used to be a woodyard kept by an old chap by the name of Capon. He had stacks of cordwood and faggots which he sold, together with manure. He also had a horse and wagon. At a date subsequent to time about which I am writing, the land occupied by this yard was built on. The houses are the first three or four at the top of the hill, the first one backing on to Harrow-road West.

I well remember this yard, as my father, when he gave himself half a day off from his usual occupation to dig and plant his garden, would go over to Mr. Priest at the garden opposite. This man was the gardener of Mr. Thorn at the large house already mentioned.

My father borrowed Mr. Priest's garden-barrow to fetch a few loads of manure from Mr. Capon's yard just above us. I accompanied him. I remember remarking it was a blessing he had to go up the hill empty, and down the hill to our gate loaded.

I would mention that at the corner on the right of the Bunkers Hill and next to the villa of the Misses Cooper, was another largish house called Hill Crest. I was not aware who occupied this house, until a date in the early 1900s when it was occupied by a Mrs. Calvert, who I think was the widow of the first incumbent of St. Paul's Church.

We will continue along the Harrow-road. There is nothing on the right-hand side that was of any interest to me other than the large villa next to a little old bungalow in a garden. The people at this villa made a high extension to the roof in order to obtain a good view of the surrounding country, and soon after this had been done a woman fell from it. I have no clear memories as to whether she was killed, whether it was suicide or pure accident, but a protective rail was soon added after the tragic fall.

Dinnage's Recollections of Old Dorking

Returning to the left hand side, after Upland Villas there came Hill View, and then Pine Cottage, the building of which is among the earliest things I can recollect in connection with this road. My mother used to take us, as quite small children, along this road - "along the top", as she called the stroll. At that time the land next to it was vacant, until some five or six years later, when two or three large villas were built. These were later absorbed into what in the end was a large convent school.

This school is a boarding as well as day school, and became very popular with many people who do not hold the Roman Catholic faith, on account of the superior education.

While writing of the convent, I will refer to the RC church fabric itself, which was not far away in Falkland-grove. I well remember the church being built, and the smaller building where the services were previously held. After the church was built, this was used as a school.

The first built places, including accommodation for the priest and those who attended to his needs, were there before the dawn of my memory, but Rev. J.S. Bright tells us they were built in 1872. [See "St. Joseph's, Dorking: A Centenary History of the Church and Parish 1872-1972" by R.F. Philpott, 1971. - Ed.]

I well remember the Rev. Father Volckeryck, the priest. He was a tall upright man, and of good proportions, with a roundish, genial, and slightly ruddy face, and hair not very thick and in no way conspicuous, just turning grey. He had a stately way of walking and wore a tall hat and always a long kind of overcoat, not of thick material.

He was reputed to be a good man and very attentive to his poorer church members. I must say I liked his appearance. I think Father Volckeryck was a Belgian, and he left Dorking after 25 years' ministry about 1903. He was followed by Father Alexander, quite a different man to my thinking, the reverse to genial.

Dinnage's Recollections of Old Dorking

The next house to what is now the convent school was Southease House, residence of Mr. Field, who I think was connected with the Metropolitan Gas Company. I can remember more vividly his son, who walked each morning to the Railway Station (LB & SCR), which we used to call in those days "The Brighton Station".

I saw him occasionally on some point of his journey thither, and he invariably wore a buttonhole of some kind in his coat.

Mr. Field also had I think three daughters, who I used to meet often in the early spring or summer mornings (when I fetched the milk from a farm, which I refer to later) taking their little dogs for a run on a lead. I think each of the ladies had a dog, and walked at a fairly brisk pace. I believe they all remained maiden ladies till their deaths, and were interested in the church at North Holmwood.

The only other house I would mention is next to the last before the road ends at Coldharbour-road. This was called Belgowan, and occupied by Mr. Harman Young. He was a fine tall military-looking man, and well fitted, I imagine, to be chosen for an officer in a military organisation called the Volunteers, which existed in those days to play a part and train for the protection of our country in conjunction with the full-blown regular army.

They had a uniform of a kind, marches, and took part in any public functions, such as took place at the processions during the celebrations of Queen Victoria's jubilees. Mr. Harman Young was the son of the owner and occupier of Stapleton House, of Brewery fame, of whom more hereafter.

We are now at the end of the Harrow-road West, and will walk to the left into the Coldharbour-road and proceed up the hill. The left side of this road had a path, and was in appearance much as in these later days of 80 years afterwards. On the right was The Nower, but without any fence to protect the sandy bank, which was broken

Dinnage's Recollections of Old Dorking

with sand falling loose at intervals along the roadside.

The fence was erected to prevent entrance to The Nower being made by climbing the bank and loosening the sand-stones which were embedded. There was a strong temptation to clamber up this bank by the boys who lived farthest away from the authorised entrance to The Nower, and I confess I for one with my boyish companions, was guilty of the sin of the gospel sheep robber by climbing up some other way, very often into the pleasant depths of the spacious Nower, where we could chase and play at many kinds of game.

As the top of the slope was reached, the bank became higher, and here was the junction where the knoll of Ridgeway-road came into the old Coldharbour-road, which continued straight on and was known by us boys as Farm-lane, until the farm was reached a quarter of a mile off. Here at this junction with the newer cut roads (Knoll and Ridgeway), was, I was told in the still older days, a gibbet, and we knew the spot in general terms of Sandy Cross.

The only house in Coldharbour-road between Harrow-road West and Sandy Cross that I would notice is the largest with a drive up to the building to the left, which were stables.

I think, when I first remember this house, it was occupied by Mr. William Attlee, of the firm of J. and W. Attlee, millers and corn merchants, of High-street, and Parsonage Mill off the Station-road near Washway.

There was a man by the name of Botting who worked for Mr. Attlee at this house in Coldharbour-road, now an annexe to Newra, as a kind of "general" man, who for a reason unknown to me rode his horse into the town on certain days of the week at about 4.30 to 5 o'clock in the afternoon, as far as my memory serves me correctly, and always (it seemed to me as a small boy) accompanied by a large dog, white and brown and somewhat curly shortish hair.

Dinnage's Recollections of Old Dorking

I was not at any time of my life a dog fancier, and never at any period or conditions squandered any affection for that class of animal, having no affection to give - on the contrary, I had rather a strong dislike of the dog tribe, expressing itself in positive fear for many years. The extra ground I covered in my earlier years to avoid close contact with dogs would amount to a number of miles.

The dog in question who ran with the horse ridden by the servant of Mr. Attlee seemed to know of the attitude I took towards his species, and whenever I met him (or her), which was on several occasions, seemed to want to stay and make my more extended acquaintance.

This I did not desire and probably made it very plain to him by quickly withdrawing myself as far from him as I could, and in fact starting to run, which he no doubt interpreted as fear of him. He repeated this desire to be better acquainted with me each time I met him until, should I be in South-street, I looked upon the approach of the horseman followed by the dog with considerable apprehension.

One day I was wearing a shortish thin overcoat, and walking along South-street, near what was then Holder House, and going towards the town, when I heard the horse coming, and knew it would soon overtake me. All at once I felt a tug at my overcoat and saw my canine, would-be friend, run past me with something in his mouth. I applied my hand to, and examined my coat, and found a very considerable gap in the back immediately covering my posterior.

I was, as one may guess, alarmed and annoyed at this, as a largish and irregular piece of material had been bitten out, and in this condition I had to make my way home and explain to my mother how I came to be in that ragged condition. Needless to say, my mother believed my tale, but I had to abandon the overcoat. I think my family were concerned as to what might have happened should I have

Dinnage's Recollections of Old Dorking

worn no overcoat and my bodily protection was only a pair of breeches!

A reader may remark that I cannot resist a digression. But even so I will go back to the Coldharbour-road, which is so closely associated with childhood days, particularly the portion we used to call Farm-lane. This terminated for us at the old Home Farm less than a quarter of a mile along towards Coldharbour.

It was the home farm of Bury Hill, residence of the Barclay family, and the public were in my early days allowed to walk along the lanes and ways to the road between the lake and the big house itself leading to the Milton Street, and Second Nower, until the privilege was stopped by Mr. Barclay at a later date.

My particular interest in this farm arose from the fact that I used to go there to get milk early on spring and summer mornings, and I can well remember the huge pans of skim milk, which were soon disposed of, for if one was not at the farm soon after six it would be a futile journey. This milk, which was liberally skimmed, was sold to us at a penny a quart, and I used to fetch it in a quart can.

The man who in those days actually occupied the farm was Neddie Neale, and we were in the habit of calling it Neale's Farm.

Milk in those early days was somewhat of a luxury and although I always had ample plain and wholesome food and meat daily, my parents remembered the days when what they called "butcher's meat" was absent six days a week from their dinner table and the flesh they consumed consisted of pork. A bit of sheep or Ox flesh was regarded as a luxury for Sundays.

I came into the world when we were first beginning to try to remedy the evils brought about by the industrial revolution, and the increasing application of machinery and steam power and the forming of the factory system by fortune-seeking men, who forgot

Dinnage's Recollections of Old Dorking

that they should pay those who helped them to prosperity a living and reasonable wage; in other words a larger share in what was produced.

Although I did not escape the days of low wages, times were improving, and, I was well housed, clothed, fed, and kept warm in winter. Milk was brought round to the door of the houses by a milkman of one of three separate purveyors trading in those days. The milk was in our district carried round in large cans, with measures hooked on. It was jolted about in these cans as the milkman walked round to his customers' houses until he had sold all the milk.

The chief call was made about 8 or 9 o'clock in the morning, though some purveyors went round in the afternoons as well. We had a very small milk-jug which held a supply which was sold for a halfpenny, and which lasted us for the day for teas.

A ha'poth of milk was our common saying - and allowance! - at one delivery. This milk was sold for new milk, so it was that access to Neale's farm for a good skim nearly as creamy as our ha'poth was, at a penny a quart, a great boon.

We will now leave Coldharbour-road and take a look at the newer roads that run into it at Sandy Cross - Ridgeway and Knoll roads. The Ridgeway-road was narrow, with very rough grass verges along its entire length, and void of houses. Knoll-road was in much the same condition but wider, and plots in that road were purchased and houses began to be built early in the 1870s.

One of the first houses I remember being built there was the one at the corner of the two newer roads, having its frontage in Knoll-road and garden boundary along Ridgeway-road. This plot was the biggest in Knoll-road which from this point ran downhill to Horsham-road.

The situation of this plot was extremely pleasant, commanding views of the expansive Nower parkland to the west; a pleasing view of the Redland Woods and country beyond

Dinnage's Recollections of Old Dorking

towards Coldharbour to the south; and glimpses of the extensive Holmwood Common. I did not, at the time it was being built, get to know the owner, but years later my wife got to know his wife very well, and she told my wife that in the early seventies, when living near London, she and her husband often came to Dorking and knew this spot in the Knoll-road quite well. They would often sit there and view and enjoy the vision of meadow, woods and parkland, and came to the decision that if ever they built a house in Dorking, a thing they had planned to do for a considerable time, it would be on this spot at the highest point of Knoll-road.

This house was built when I was a small boy and the owners lived there for many years; in fact until their deaths. The name of this gentleman was Alfred Chabot, who died a nonagenarian, and he named his new home "Viewlands".

Mr. Chabot laid out a large part of his garden on the north and west sides as a kind of rockery, of an original and unique kind, introducing fragments of old brick and stone and statuary from old buildings. "Viewlands" was built at the time when the old church of St. Martin's was taken down and rebuilt in the early 1870s, and materials for this novel ornamentation of the garden were largely selected from fragmentary portions of masonry and statuary belonging to the old church.

Leaving "Viewlands", we descend the hill down to Horsham-road. Building continued to go on in Knoll-road for some years, and most of the houses were erected on the left hand side - on the right hand, next to "Viewlands", there was an open space filled with rough bushes and shrubs, part belonging to "Viewlands" and part to the house next door soon to be erected by Mr. James Todman, who lived there until his death, and his wife.

As we reach the Horsham turnpike road, we will turn to the left, and soon find ourselves at the bottom of the East and West Harrow-roads again. Before we leave the

Dinnage's Recollections of Old Dorking

turnpike at this, the southern portion, I should like to write a few words about the old toll-gate, or as we who lived within sight of it knew it - the pay gate.

This I remember quite well. It stood a few yards south of the "Bush Inn" and across the road, on the right hand side going south, was the Toll Keeper's Cottage, and a gate for pedestrians spanned the path on the left.

I went through this toll-gate on several occasions in a conveyance. A kind relation on a visit to my parents would often take us for a drive, and we most often went in the direction of the Holmwood. There were two "jobmasters" (as people who kept private carriages and horses were called), quite close to where I lived. Mr. Mat Napper had a large carriage and stables a few paces from the toll-gate on Dorking town side, and there was another jobmaster with a smaller business, old Mr. Harding, at the Queen's Head public house.

Mat Napper had a daughter who drove a pony in a four-wheeled low chaise. Several old ladies who lived in lodgings in the neighbourhood of the old toll-gate were driven for a gentle run along the old country lanes by her.

Mr. Charlie Shearman, a man of some note in Dorking and surrounding villages, lived near where the old pay-gate stood, and at the time about which I am writing, sold tea and tobacco in a small way. I well remember on rare occasions, when my father was having a few hours away from his usual business to tend his garden, being told by him to run and get a half-ounce of tobacco from Mr. Shearman, whom he knew quite well. I remember it was always Mitcham Shag, and he entrusted me with 2d. for the purchase.

Mr. Shearman was, I think, a "branch plucked from the burning" and had considerable religious fervour. He held meetings in surrounding villages as well as taking his trade there. He prospered and opened a shop in Falkland-road, selling tea, tobacco and confectionery. He acquired two light carts and

Dinnage's Recollections of Old Dorking

horses on which he conveyed his merchandise to the outlying districts.

The Prince of Wales, in Hampstead-road, which has been altered since my young days was a far less imposing house with "Fine Sparkling Ales and London Porter" in large letters painted across the front of the building. Houses and a shop have since been built towards the Horsham-road end.

A large house, known as Orchard House, was situated charmingly in Hampstead-road. Where the cottages and shop now stand was part of the ornamental grounds with evergreen shrubs and trees. A flint wall surrounded the grounds, forming a nice curved corner into the Horsham turnpike road.

The house opposite, now an attractive grocers, was I well remember kept by a lady by the name of Goble. She did mangling for those women - and it was most in those days - for those who did not possess mangles of their own. She also sold gingerbread, which was kept in her window - it seemed to me for several weeks.

My parents told me that this house was the first built in the road by the husband of the lady who sold gingerbread, having accumulated over the years enough material to build the house. He gathered the materials for the house - big stones, flints and brickbats - where he could and stored them on the site. He was a pie-man and died before I was born.

Now we will take a look in the northerly direction, and should enter Dorking town itself, via South-street. From the pay-gate and walking a few dozen paces further on, we reach the East and West Harrow-roads, one each side of the turnpike; a little further on, on the right, Orchard-road, and a few paces still further a bank began. By ascending a short flight of steps, one gained access to a cornfield, with a path running through it and leading out over a stile to a lane which led to St. Paul's-road, close to the church.

Dinnage's Recollections of Old Dorking

The stile was close to some steps leading up to the cottage hospital - built about a decade before my recollections begin, and which greeted my baby eyes every time I went to the top of our garden. The path in the cornfield was nearly along a line followed by the road as it is today, with Cliftonville on the left.

The old lane at the top is today much as it was then, 85 years ago, and looking through the old hedge on the left hand side on the ground now occupied by the county hospital, in bygone days could be seen a group of boys assembled in their playground clad in light corduroy, and the juvenile paupers of the workhouse. I cannot remember much about the garb of the girls and women. Their duties no doubt kept them more out of public view, and they were not, I think, allowed to stroll out of the grounds. Certainly if they were married, with husbands as inmates, they were made to live the life of grass widows. The men likewise, if married, were not able to continue any domestic happiness to which they may have been used.

The field that was developed into Cliftonville was not all arable land. The part bordering on what is now the Orchard-road was meadowland, and a cowshed stood near the upper corner. I used to see the labourer arrive each afternoon at 4 o'clock to take the cow into the shed for milking. I was not awake when morning milking would be done. My mother told me that when she called on the person with a view to taking No. 7 Hampstead-road (then Briar Cottage), where I was born, my mother was told: "She's up the field blackberrying!" Cliftonville was cut to form a circle, finishing in a single road at the bottom. The steps were taken away together with the old field surface and bank, to finish at Horsham turnpike level - hence the extra steep gradient at the entrance into Horsham-road.

The house at the end of the road in Cliftonville, running parallel with Horsham-road and at the top of the bank, was occupied for a time by Grant Allen, the novelist

Dinnage's Recollections of Old Dorking

and writer of articles on science and wild life. He entertained some men of note, George MacDonald and I think Herbert Spencer and Matthew Arnold among others. I often saw Grant Allen (whom I could recognise by his "walk") in the town and lanes. His house was named "The Nook".

Going back to the turnpike, we soon reach the cutting, which is much as it was years ago, although a little less wild on the western side. This bit of road was called The Hollow - "The Holler" to the youngsters.

Once a horse grazing in the meadow at the top of the high bank ventured too near the edge of the field and fell into the road, sustaining injuries which necessitated his having to be put to sleep. The animal belonged to a Falkland-road butcher, but I never learned whether he sold horse flesh.

When I was quite young I saw the heavy carts bringing flints - I think mostly from Ranmore Common - and tipping them into the middle of the road, at intervals, to be spread. This was all that was done. There were no steam-rollers in those days and the iron tyres of carts, vans and carriages ground them into the road surface. As a result, the dust was terrific in the summer, and water carts went round to lay it. In the winter the mud was appalling and the Local Board (I suppose it was) sent their men with wide rakes to clear off the mud and place it in heaps by the roadside. This was repeated at intervals throughout the winter.

Bad for rubber tyres? I remember seeing an occasional carriage with rubber-solid, of course - on the iron tyres. The cartman who got the contract for the job of fetching flints in those days was a man named Harry Knight.

Horsham-road has altered little since I first remember it, excepting at the part adjoining South-street where the bus garage now stands. Here there was a mansion called "Townfield" approached by a short coach road from the main road. The kitchen gardens were on the opposite side of the Horsham-road, the road being then narrower than at present and a

Dinnage's Recollections of Old Dorking

tarred cleft pale fence ran along next to the path, dividing the property from the public road.

At the corner where St. Paul's-road turns out of Horsham-road were the coach house and stables belonging to Townfield. Comparatively new houses now occupy the land which was once the gardens and the then vacant meadowland further up St. Paul's-road, on both sides. An old field gate near the turning from the main road on the right-hand side up the incline led into the meadow where horses and sheep were often grazing.

Dinnage's Recollections of Old Dorking

South Street area

When the newer houses were built to replace the old ones, the shop now the "Mad Hatter" was opened as a chemists. I can just remember one of the old houses having a gun shop, but cannot recall the name of the man who sold and repaired the guns. Opposite was the Queen's Head, kept by Mr. Harding, who also owned a landau and was a jobmaster in a small way. A road divided the Queen's Head yard from the baker's shop, kept at one time by Mr. Charlie Hoad, whom the wags sometimes described as the "Moonlight Baker".

Next, going into South-street was the old red brick house, demolished in more recent years on the site of May's Garage. Probably built in the days of Queen Anne, it was a house that helped to give the town of Dorking an old-world kind of aspect; one of a type fast now disappearing.

One of the vicars of St. Martin's, the Rev. George Feacham, vicar 1800-1837, lived in the house for a time and it was known as "The Old Vicarage", but was never the vicarage officially.

On the left-hand side of South-street, when I was a boy, the building lying back from the road and known as the Bartholomew Press, was the building works carried on by Mr. Wm. Shearburn. A large number of men were employed at these works, and the time of departure and arrival was announced to them - and most of the inhabitants of the town - by a loud whistle. "Shearburn's whistle" was often a time regulator for non-employees at the south end of the town.

Dinnage's Recollections of Old Dorking

The firm of Shearburn built the present Congregational Church and the workhouse. Another familiar sound was what we called the "Union Bell", which sounded to give notice for the workhouse inmates to assemble for meals.

Next to Shearburn's yard in South-street was a florist's establishment with a greenhouse of considerable length running back from the street. The business belonged to Mr. Harry Lucas, who also kept pigs, and had another large garden, where houses have now been built. This is now Vincent-drive. Flowers, I think, were grown there.

Mr. Lucas lived next to the big greenhouse in the house with the well-designed porch. A two-wheeled cart and horse was kept for collecting the swill. This was collected in a large-size can, something like a milk-can, let through the floor of the cart.
Mr. Lucas' legs terminated in gaiters, which he wore a little over his strong boots. He looked exceedingly grave and unhandsome when he essayed to run after the boys who, for reasons I never knew, called him "Pickle Breeches".

A few paces further on was the "Old House", where a medical practice was carried out by Dr. Brock, whose brother was a curate of St. Martin's Church.

The house with a window now displaying modern tents was in my earlier days a private house, and the wide road leading off South-street into the back of the premises had iron gates giving access to what was then a large meadow. This meadow extended right to Vincent-lane, where the Powell Corderoy School was afterwards built.

I read lately the book written by Mr. Cousin on the British School, in which I am especially interested, being an old boy myself. This is what I remember of my school days there in Church-street. I did not begin my schooling there, but as I was deemed too old at about 9 or 10 to continue at a Dame School, my parents decided to send me to a larger one.

Dinnage's Recollections of Old Dorking

They could not decide at once whether it would be to St. Paul's, where most of our neighbours' children attended, or the British. I recall my father taking me to see Mr. Pithard, headmaster of St. Paul's, but cannot remember any details of the interview. My father evidently was not impressed by the short contact with St. Paul's, or its headmaster.

I think probably he did not relish his son being under the influence of the Church of England, as he was a member of the Congregational Church, and so it was decided to send me to the British School which was free from creed.

So one morning I accompanied my father to the old British School in Church-street, and saw the headmaster, Mr. Reeves, there. I felt very nervous. He was a man on the stout side with nearly black hair parted in the middle, side whiskers, short beard, and a moustache, and was of slightly less than middle height. I think he hailed from Bristol. He did not often smile, but on the occasions when he did he showed some fine white teeth. I put his age at about 40.

We met him at the entrance to a classroom from the playground and my father introduced me as a late pupil of a Dame School. After asking my age, Mr. Reeves seemed most interested in my advance in arithmetic, asking what sums I had been doing. Mrs. Croucher, my late mistress, did not teach arithmetic (at least so I thought) with very great aptitude and clearness, but I had lately been introduced to sums of £ s d, addition and subtraction and was just struggling with multiplication.

So I told Mr. Reeves I was doing "Money Sums" at which I remember he smiled. He agreed to take me and so about the end of March, 1880, I started and was put into Standard IV.

There were in the school at that time three pupil-teachers. Arthur Dewdney, who afterwards became a Baptist minister, went to New Zealand and was eventually President of the Union there; Mr. Nehemiah Croucher, son of

Dinnage's Recollections of Old Dorking

a greengrocer in South-street; and Miss Una Maber, daughter of the barber in High-street. I knew Mr. Dewdney very well, and went to his house in Roses Cottages for books which he lent me. He preached at the Congregational Church years later when on a visit from New Zealand.

Miss Maber was the teacher of Standards III and IV, through which I passed, and I think got on well with her boys, though I cannot record that I was fascinated with her ways and looks. She was small and with a round face, and I think seldom smiled. She was always fair when any unpleasantness arose among the boys. Her method was to teach by constant repetition, and she pointed round the map of England endlessly. At school we were not supposed to be interested in any countries except those coloured red. In later days I had to learn of other countries on my own initiative.

I remember the meadow in South-street as it was used each Whit-Monday, as far as my memory serves - a Bank Holiday anyway - for the carrying on of a fete. The entrance was at the gates in South-street and the field, I think, was known as "Fuller's Field". Mr. Fuller lived for a time in the house already mentioned, now the Pneumatic Tent Co's offices.

A payment was made to enter the fete, for various forms of entertainment were available. It was something like a small fair. The chief attraction, at any rate to the writer of these notes, was the ascent of a balloon. The silken cover was inflated with coal gas, until ready to carry the passengers. It was held to the ground by strong cords fastened by, I think, stakes and swung to and fro calmly and with great dignity.

When ready to start, the large basket-car was entered by Mr. Hendon, who was a local aeronaut, and I think a Mr. Hickman. It sailed away, gradually rising higher as it passed over the town, watched by the crowd until it was out of sight. Mr. Hickman kept a bookshop in the High-street, before the arrival of Mr. Doubleday, who carried on a

Dinnage's Recollections of Old Dorking

chemists business then for a good number of years, and was very popular and successful.

It appeared to me that the fetes were due largely to initiative of Mr. Jack Sanford, who at one time had the honour of being the Town Crier.

Passing along the short distance, we come to the butcher's shop - which in those days sold nothing but meat. It was then run by a man whose name was Jenkins, being taken over later by Mr. F.F. Tracey, who greatly improved the appearance of the exterior of the shop. Mr. Tracey will be known to many now living in the town.

Next to this shop was the entrance to the slaughter house, and then, where the Wesleyan schoolroom now stands, a couple of old stone cottages including one which was the home of a fly proprietor by the name of Emery Dawes. At the rear of the premises he kept his flys and carriages, and there were also stables for his horses. Later in his business life he ran a bus, which met trains at the South Eastern Railway Co's station, and which was then, and some years after his time, a more or less regular service, conveying people from the town to the station, or vice versa.

The bus was in the last days of its service driven by Mr. King. Speaking of horse buses, there was one earlier still run by Mr. Swift of the "Three Tuns Hotel". This was a heavier and rather more cumbersome affair, and had a door at the back. This 'bus also served the South Eastern Co's station.

Where the Methodist Church now stands, there lived and worked a tradesman and his wife by the name of Johnson. We called the man Jimmie Johnson and his trade and occupation was that of coal and wood merchant.
Mrs. Johnson kept a shop, selling confectionery and a small assortment of toys, including whips and spinning tops, and tallow candles which gave their scent pretty often to the entire shop.

The shop was entered through a door which was divided into two, the upper half usually kept

Dinnage's Recollections of Old Dorking

open. It may have been to keep the shop free from the too predominating smells! Over the shop window was a heavy tiled covering, or porch.

Mrs. Johnson was a good specimen of womanhood as regards bodily build and not too athletic. She emerged from the more private sanctum of her dwelling when she became aware of one's presence in the shop, and after she fully understood what was wanted by the customer, would very slowly and carefully proceed to procure it.

Mr. Jimmie Johnson gave the impression, at least to me as a youngster, of being kindly and even-tempered. On Saturday afternoons he went the rounds of Falkland-road and Hampstead-road (he had a competitor in the former) and also extended his services supplying fuel to the cottages to the growing Orchard-road.

From the top of Orchard-road he would take a number of boys into his two four-wheel vans, being now empty of coal and wood, and convey the boys to his yard in South-street. The ride was compensation for the effort of walking back.

The yard at the back, extending some distance, was used for the stabling of his horses, van sheds, and stores of coal, wood and chips for firelighting. The chips, made when clearing coopers' hoops in the coppices, were 2½d. and 3d. per bundle, and would light a dozen or more fires of the parlour cottage type. Mr. Johnson cut his large wood by means of a circular saw, the driving power being derived from one of his horses which was driven round a circular path connected to a long horizontal iron rod, which was in some way cogged up to the saw spindle. Size of the firewood was just convenient for the cottage grates.

The view from the narrow entry into Vincent-road was at that time of day markedly different from the present aspect. One could see only the large field referred to earlier, and the upland pastures on the west side of

Dinnage's Recollections of Old Dorking

Vincent-lane, where sheep grazed in serenity and peace.

Norfolk-road had not then been cut, and the school buildings were yet to come. There was no Nower-road and the sand since dug out was still in its primitive state, reposing under the pasture of grazing sheep.

On the opposite side of the narrow lane to the coal yard was a small market garden kept by Mr. Ford, who was often to be seen standing at the entrance to his plot.

I must not omit to mention the partly ivy-clad old cottage standing opposite the wood yard of Mr. Johnson in bygone years. It occupied a good part of the ground where the "Pavilion" now stands, and was within the high stone wall, which extended somewhat further than at present. The ground on which the cottage stood was higher than the public road, South-street, and was approached through a gate in or at the end of the stone wall, and then up a few steps.

This cottage was the residence of a Miss Reeve, who kept a girls' school. I remember Miss Reeve as a lady getting on towards the evening of life, of pleasant manner, and whose iron-grey hair hung in ringlets over and below her ears.

Next to this cottage, and between it and Holder House, was the building used by Mr. John Jeal, the carrier to London. Very large doors opened to admit the vans into a big barn-like space at the road level, and from inside this large and high part of the house which accommodated certain of the vans when not in use, a flight of wooden steps led to the living rooms (built above the ground floor of the van shelter) where Mr. John Jeal and his family lived. The stables were behind the main building in South-street. Mr. Jeal conveyed goods to and from London on certain days of each week, assisted by a faithful and steady type of man by the name of Tom Elms.

Just as one left the yard gates of the last mentioned premises, in a small recess next to Holder House, a blind fruit and sweet seller

Dinnage's Recollections of Old Dorking

was allowed to station himself in a very small hut in which he could retreat if necessary or store his little stock. He used to sit on a camp stool with his basket of goods (mostly oranges) below him. He was John Skilton, known as "Blind John", and he was of a very Godly turn of mind, and attended the services of Miss Cotton, mentioned earlier.

"Blind John" was previously allowed a footing at the top of Junction-road. Holder House was entirely residential and stood back about three feet from the pavement. A post and chains fence ran along the outer boundary.

What is now the property of the Guildford Co-operative Society, the old cinema, and the redbrick private house, was in my younger days the residence of John Young, a gentleman who was connected with a firm of brewers. The brewery was situated on the land which is now known as Myrtle-road. At about the entrance to this road, and standing back somewhat from Back-lane (now Church-street) and opposite "The Plat" was a large house, which before my time must have been a very imposing and important one, probably the residence of one of the family of Youngs. It was known as Myrtle House.

Coming back to South-street, the house in which John Young lived was known as Stapleton House. I remember the garden and land at the back was higher than now. The society that bought the property dug out a large quantity of valuable sand and reduced the level considerably. This can be seen by looking at the height of the wall dividing the Co-op property from that belonging to the Society of Friends. When the Friends' Meeting House was built in 1846, a quantity of sand was dug out under the property of Stapleton House making a deep cave, which was used by the Friends by the sanction of the owner. It was very large and useful as storage for fruit, coal and wood. But the Co-operative Society, when digging their sand also dug out the cave.

At the top of Butter Hill, opposite the present gates of the Friends Meeting House, stood

Dinnage's Recollections of Old Dorking

a very old cottage, and on the same side was next a shoe shop, kept by Fred Lee - "Prouts patent dubbing" seemed to be the most prominent advertisement in his windows. Wooden barns came next, and last, the home of Mr. Spratley, afterwards replaced by a more important house and shop also kept by members of the Spratley family.

Facing South-street, where Victoria-terrace now stands, next to Stapleton House, was another moderately large house, and the ground towards the meeting house was vacant. This house was before I can remember occupied by a Rev. John Whitehouse, Minister of the Congregational Church, and many years earlier by the Rev. John Mason, also of that church, so my mother told me, and in my very early days one of the policemen, Tugwell by name.

The police station was then stationed near where now the public lavatories are situated. There was also the "Lock Up", a small building to house the fire engine, and the fire bell hung at the top of a square shaft. I can well remember Superintendent Lambert living at the house, a part of the police station building, and have seen the inspectors of weights and measures at work there in the public interest.

The South-street of that time was narrower than now, and a much higher wall formed the boundary of the public road on the eastern side. The causeway at the top of the wall, which ran as now, was wider, and larger trees than now grew on the South-street side.

The narrow lane leading from South-street on the west side leading to Roses Cottages, and Cat's Fields, was called Chopstick-place. The large house (in which the Dorking Advertiser offices are now situated) was for many years the residence of Dr. Paxon. I remember this gentleman - who I think did most of his visiting on foot - always suggested to my mind the face and figure of Mr. Pickwick. My parents told me that Dr. Paxon did take part, with considerable acceptance, in what was called the "Penny Readings", that were given in a room at "The Red Lion" at near intervals.

No doubt the Pickwick Papers were read, and Dr. Paxon would, I imagine, be the right

Dinnage's Recollections of Old Dorking

person to read the illustrious doings of Mr. Pickwick and his friends. The practice carried on by Dr. Paxon transferred to the care of the doctor living in the modern house built in what was once a part of the Stapleton estate, and nearly opposite to "Chopstick Place". Next to his house were others, the first occupied by, I think, the first resident agent of the Singer Sewing Machine Company. The agency was announced by a large board over the door, or near it. The agent was one Girling by name, and he or his wife were successful in selling my mother a sewing machine!

A few paces further on was the shop known for a good many years as a builders, or more strictly as a decorators and plumbers, owned by Bargman & Sons. When I was quite tiny, but just old enough to retain an impression of things I saw, the site was a bit of rough grassland, enclosed (if that is the term) by a rough fence in very bad repair.

The plot was used for religious meetings, I was told, and I can remember seeing a crowd of people assembled there. I have been told that a short religious mission was held there under canvas and the then famous evangelist, Henry Moorhouse, conducted a service in what is now Junction-road, then sometimes called New-road. It was in those days in a very stony, rutty and uneven condition.

The carpenter's and joinery shop on the left-hand side of the road a distance down was then in the hands of a Mr. Heselgrove. This gentleman I think lived in the villa next door, and was a man in my young days of very goodly proportions. He attended the Congregational Church, and so did I, sitting not very far behind him, and on his arrival at Divine Service, I well remember that I had fears as to the capacity of the seat, as it creaked considerably as he slowly committed his full weight to it.

An old private house occupied the site of the block of new buildings running into Junction-road and facing South-street, and part of the old building projected into South-street, and was adapted at some time

Dinnage's Recollections of Old Dorking

to comprise a shop kept by a Mr. Jones, who was a baker and confectioner. This shop stood next to a private house pulled down to accommodate a drapery shop.

This old, and rather picturesque Wyngate House was for a long time the home of Mr. W.J. Rossiter, whose ironmongery business was carried on in the High-street before being taken over by Mr. Chas. Peirson. Mr. Rossiter was for 16 years vicar's warden, of St. Martin's Church. He it was who, in April 1877, laid the top stone of the spire of the present parish church. The Rev. Neville Stiff gives a few notes of the event in his book published in 1912.

Next came the "Spotted Dog" and part of the inn as at present seen was a newspaper and stationery shop kept by Mrs. Borer before removing to the shop opposite the "Bull's Head" inn. A passing memory must be inserted, of the proprietors of the "Spotted Dog".

The earliest recollection I have is that the name of the proprietors was Greathurst, and it was for a long time in the capable hands of Miss Greathurst, the last survivor of that name. A booth from this inn supplied refreshments on Derby Day at Epsom, and I can remember the wagon filled with the necessary gear to erect the booth, standing in front of the inn a day or so before it was due to be drawn to Epsom in time for the "Races".

One of the gentlemen who then lived at the "Spotted Dog" was known as Jack Greathurst, and he with another gentleman by the name of Walter Whaley were the most popular members of a troop formed of a number of more or less talented men of the town into what they were pleased to call the "ICU Minstrels".

I have never gathered whether this name stood for any words, or whether selected as ephonious initials. However, Jack Greathurst was a great wit and the "ICU Minstrels" would, I believe, have been less sparkling if he had withdrawn his enthusiasm. The question master, the only man who did not black his face, was Mr. Ison, the popular relieving

Dinnage's Recollections of Old Dorking

officer, who lived in the house next to "The Cricketers" in South-street on the south side. The troop placarded the public Bill-sticking boards in the town, notably, that at the top of Station-road, with large lettered notices: "The ICU Minstrels are Coming" when they were presenting their show.

Jack Greathurst was much sought after as a reciter and popular entertainer by various institutions. These were the days when a number of companies of play artists visited the town, and gave performances in the large room of the public hall for perhaps a week.

A very well patronised entertainment was Poole's Diorama. The first picture was generally the central offices of the Prudential Insurance Company, in High Holborn, London - a good advertisement! The moving rollers along which the pictures unfolded along the stage were stopped at intervals to vary the scene and to lessen the strain on the audience in taking the tour round the world. For this a brief performance of something in the way of song, conjuring or dancing was given, or a Ventriloquist would appear. This happened several times during the tour.

Getting back to South-street, the shop now a chemists was in the '80s a barber's shop, where Mr. Wilson cut one's hair for twopence, and would shave you for one penny. There was, and is I suppose (but not so much today) talk by the assembled customers on current topics. I am wondering whether the subject of inflation was one of them!

It was at this shop, I remember, I made my first acquaintance with Mr. Robert Spratley, who some years later acquired the hairdresser's business in High-street, succeeding Mr. Caffyn. The name of this gentleman may be better known by the work of his accomplished son who was a local artist of great talent and repute. Mr. Caffyn had been a county cricketer - the famous England player was his brother.

Next comes the printers and bookbinders establishment, the proprietor of which was for many years Mr. Charles Rowe - who was

Dinnage's Recollections of Old Dorking

also a member of the Dorking Voluntary Fire Brigade.

There was a high-class china shop next door, kept by some ladies by the name of Randall.

Opposite, when South-street was a much narrower thoroughfare than now, was the fish shop kept by Mr. Tugwell. When the widening and remodelling of this part of the street was carried out, this business was transferred by a successor of Mr. Tugwell to the opposite side of the street where it still exists. The earlier shop of Mr. C. Spratley, a stationer and newsagent, was where the boot and shoe shop now (when this article was written) does business.

I well remember the display of "Police News", which attracted the public attention to the shop window as large pictures of the doings of burglars and murderers were given great prominence; to note one whose name has become immortal, Mr. Charles Peace!

Here in this window and shop were innumerable Valentines in full splendour a week or two before February 14. These were of the more comic type and highly coloured.

I have heard that this shop was once entered by the Rev. Chas. Haddon Spurgeon, of the Tabernacle, Newington Butts, London, who published his sermons weekly at a penny a copy. Buying one himself, he asked the wife of the proprietor who was serving customers, if she sold many copies. She did not recognise the gentleman as Mr. Spurgeon, the author, as she was not a strict devotee to any religious denomination, and told him the sale was very poor.

The large grocers kept by Mr. Butler has been referred to, and came next on the left side of South-street. A licence was allowed to this grocer, and this was a boon for customers who preferred to take their stimulants in seclusion, a privilege and facility conferred by Mr. Gladstone, I think. The beer barrels were kept in the Rotunda opposite the shop, the space now occupied by shops.

Dinnage's Recollections of Old Dorking

The grocery business passed first to Mr. Portsmouth, and then to Messrs. Cole and Adams.

The draper's business then belonging to Mr. Charles Rose is still in existence under the proprietorship of Mr. Chas. Degenhardt, and now extends to part of the site on which the grocer's shop stood. Mr. Rose contributed in 1875 a number of "Recollections of Dorking" to a Guildford local weekly, which were afterwards published in book form.

A tailor's was next to the "White Lion" public house. The tailor was Mr. Joyce, who was the conductor and probably the instigator of a decent and efficient fife and drum band, which often paraded the streets of Dorking, giving wholesome employment for the minds of many of the youths of the town.

The "White Lion" was kept by Mr. Mills who also, I think, was a member of the troop of the ICU Minstrels.

We have now reached what was called the "Pump Corner". Behind the pump stood, and still stands, a confectionery shop, then kept by a Mr. Brown. Subsequent traders here were Rix, Wickman, and now Loyns. Mr. Brown in those days also had a licence to sell wines, and I think many found it more in keeping with their respectability to take the vintage from "Browns".

No doubt the town pump was a major source of water for the inhabitants around before the water works system was instituted. Another source of supply was a spring enclosed in a small bricked cavity, down a step or two, situated close to the turning into Spring-gardens from Station-road. Another spring existed at the lower end of Mill-lane near the old "Evening Star".

Before the monopoly of the People's Drink was the method of distribution and manufacture of beer, there were three breweries in the town, and one was near the spring in Mill-lane and known as Boxalls Brewery. Another was Young's, before mentioned, and a third was carried on by Messrs. Lucock at a site in High-street. There was also a

Dinnage's Recollections of Old Dorking

public house, I think kept by one or more members of the brewery firm, and known as "The Rock".

I well recollect, being on occasions in the High-street and passing near the entrance to the Rock Brewery, seeing the Lucocks and their men bringing out the open grains in large basket containers and tipping them into farm wagons drawn alongside the high pavement and approached by planks from the pavement to the sides of the wagon. The men wore red caps, and the scent of the grains to me was delicious!

Next to Brown's the cake shop (now Loyns), before one turned sharp left into West-street, there was a small draper's shop kept by Fielder Bros. They were enterprising, and soon after much enlarged their premises by moving over to the shops one of which has been occupied by Jerome, the hairdressers, for a good number of years.

I have a dim recollection that the houses the large block replaced were a continuation of the one then occupied by Mr. Arthur Fuller, the butcher, for many years. Mr. Fielder's shop took all the block. He was a draper, clothier, and sold boots and shoes. The vacated shop behind the pump was afterwards carried on by Mr. Franklin as a furniture and upholstery business.

Passing across the top of West-street, we should in those days have noted a large draper's shop. This continued down West-street as a clothiers, and was kept by W.A. Marsh, and later by the Tebb brothers.

Dinnage's Recollections of Old Dorking

High Street area

Walking across the entrance of North-street to the High-street, we should arrive at the Post Office. The entrance and letter box was in High-street.

Dorking Post Office in those days did not employ a post-master, but was in the charge of a postmistress, Miss Lanham, daughter of the previous postmaster, a very obliging and helpful person who was greatly helped, I think, by another lady by the name of Miss Beves. This lady's father kept a clock-maker's shop in West-street.

Next to the Post Office, before reaching the entrance to the "King's Head Yard" was a printer's shop kept by a Mr. Simmonds.

A musical instrument seller by the name of Churchill was for some time the next which would be noted. Mr. Churchill was the organist at the old Wesleyan Church. The organ there was a powerful American type, and not until the new church in South-street was built did that worthy and distinguished religious body have a pipe church organ.

Then came Jackie Maber, the barber. He had a pole outside his shop, indicating his trade, as barber's did long after other trades signs had disappeared.

There was a large grocer's shop next, Jackies - the Golden Canister, kept by Robert Pearce, and I well remember a huge model metal tea can, or chest, standing on a level with the upper windows of the house, above the shop entrance. He was succeeded by F.W. Floyd.

Mr. Ashworth had an office which was in the nature of a small estate agent's business, I think between the last mentioned grocers and the wine and spirit shop kept by Mr. Joseph Maybank. Mr. Ashworth collected cottage rents and by his deportment was very successful. Above his offices existed for a time a working men's club, and Mr. Ashworth acted as secretary. Mr. Maybank was a

Dinnage's Recollections of Old Dorking

member of the local council in his later years, and an active supporter of Shrove Tuesday football.

A wide space between this wine shop and the next led to Cape Place, where existed some very old cottages, long ago demolished.
Mr. John Chart occupied the shop on the eastern side of Cape Place. He was a cabinet maker and upholsterer, and also undertaker. I think he was often successful in obtaining the contracts for the burial of the workhouse paupers from the Board of Guardians of the Poor.

The pauper corpses were conveyed to the Dorking Cemetery in a two-wheeled hearse drawn by one horse. Of course in those days, in the interests of the rate-payers, every economy had to be considered and there was a great saving of unnecessary furniture and embellishments of which the successful undertakers were fully aware. They carried out the melancholy work accordingly.

The jewellers and watchmakers establishment next was carried on by Mr. James Hubbard, who was a member of the Dorking Voluntary Fire Brigade. He had two sons and I remember one of them was one of the first to entrust his life to a pennyfarthing bicycle. He was tall and the larger of the wheels was pretty tall too! Among others of the bicycle heroes of the time was Mr. Alloway, a son of Mr. George Alloway the dignified rate collector.

Mr. Thomas Wood had his large grocer's shop next, still going east. This establishment is now known as Kinghams and was transferred to the present premises, formerly those of Mr. Robert Pearce already referred to. The large clock then stood over the original shop.

Mr. R.T. Clark, a printer, bookseller and publisher came next. I think this is now represented by the business of W.H. Smith and Sons. Mr. W. Cole the leather cutter, and his daughter were always to be seen in the next establishment. He sold hides for soles, leather for uppers and all things necessary for the shoe-making trade, including pelts,

Dinnage's Recollections of Old Dorking

brads, laces, and general grinding. In those days hand-made footwear was in great demand, and there were several efficient cord wainers in the town.

Next to what was called the Church Pavement was the old-established land and estate agents, Messrs. Alexander and Archibald White, subsequently White and Sons.

Part of the house on the eastern side of Church Pavement projected over it forming an arch or covered way from the High-street. Next came the chemist's shop which was kept by a Mr. Durant, who I think also acted as a dentist.

Mr. Durant did his best as regards skill, I'm told, although his instruments no doubt have since been improved upon. Sufferers of those days were not too eager to sit in his chair!

"The Sun" and "Three Tuns" were going strong in my young days and an additional public house, almost next door to the latter and known as the "Black Horse" also catered for certain of the thirsty inhabitants of the town. This last mentioned has passed out of existence.

Mill-lane in those days led to Boxalls Brewery mentioned already, and on the left-hand side going north were some old cottages of a slummy aspect and entered by a step down from the lane. For many years a good-class photographer's establishment was kept there by Mr. Usherwood, who previously had his business in the Falkland-road area, and on the same side of the road as the Falkland School.

I remember being taken to Mr. Usherwood to have my portrait taken when very young and wondering why that gentleman had to display a number of toys before his sitters, and what the object had to do with the production of the picture of me which he was supposed to be taking. There were no very rapid films in those days.

Mr. Usherwood left Falkland-road and established himself in the house past the entrance into Mill-lane, and there did a good trade

Dinnage's Recollections of Old Dorking

for a number of years. After a time it was taken over by Mr. Moorhouse, and then demolished for the erection of the emporium known as "Woolworths". There were some private houses after we passed the furniture and upholsterers shop occupied by Mr. Frank Davey, who also was an undertaker.

About opposite the "Surrey Yeoman" was, when I was quite young, the last business house of the southern side of East-street - then so-called. It was a coach builder's works owned by Mr. Walker. These shops and buildings were on the edge of the meadow which is now the Wathen estate, streets and houses known as Wathen, Hart and Rothes roads.

Further east was the attractive nursery garden kept by Mr. Ivery. The public were allowed to walk through these gardens, entering somewhere near what is now the court house and leaving the gardens near what is now the end of Rothes-road as it joins the London-road.

A large residence called Lonsdale House was situated next to the entrance to Ivery's Nursery to the east, and between the latter and this private house stood some large trees. Beyond Lonsdale House was another residence called Ivy Holt standing behind a flint wall immediately on the left-hand bend into London-road.

The opposite side of the road was Moores-road, and on the west corner was a private boarding school kept by Mr. John Box. He was formerly master of the British School before my time, and a man of scholarly attainments. He was an attendant of the Independent Chapel (Congregational Church) and his school boarders were taken there on Sunday mornings and sat in long pews facing the side of the ample pulpit.

Mr. John Box was an asset to the church of those days, rendering service as a capable reader of a large men's Bible class, and able expositor of scripture in other departments of church life. He was, too, somewhat of a poet, publishing two volumes of poems - one an epic entitled "The Deluge" and another "Cloe and Cloie".

Dinnage's Recollections of Old Dorking

I do not think these poems had a very large circulation, and I cannot find any reference to them in these latest times. I fear they may have gone the way of the ones produced by the genius of Robert Montgomery, but without the aid of Macaulay, rather than the way of the poems of the earlier poet, John Milton.

From the boarding school of John Box to the "Surrey Yeoman" opposite the Wathen estate there existed a high brick wall enclosing the house and estate of Lady Elizabeth Jane Wathen, daughter of the late Earl of Rothes.

The pathway was much higher than the road on that - the southern - side, and protected by a continuous wood post and iron chain fence on the roadside edge.

Quoting from a handbook of Dorking published in 1855, the author says: "The grounds attached to the house are laid out with considerable taste, and afford ample scope, by the undulations of the land for all the mysteries of landscape gardening. They are bounded by Cotmandene, a beautiful and healthy common of about 12 acres in extent, and a favourite resort of cricketers during the summer months, and pleasant promenade at all times for the soil is dry and the air fresh and breezy, and the view of the surrounding country beautiful exceedingly".

The estate and house was called "Shrub Hill". The site of the tall houses now fronting Cotmandene was then part of the estate, and between the gardens of these houses and the wall referred to in East-street, the land has been levelled and adapted to the rear of the line of shops in what is now called High-street.

The first shop built and occupied on the east side of the "Surrey Yeoman" was that of artist and musician brothers named Dawes. One painted pictures and the other sold musical instruments and copies of scripts, songs, and general accessories relating to the musical profession. The business was afterwards acquired by a Guildford firm by the name of Andrews and Court, who removed later to South-street.

Dinnage's Recollections of Old Dorking

I cannot attempt to give the names of the shopkeepers along the south side of the High-street in earlier days, or the designation of all the shops, but would mention the "Ram Inn" as a fairly old-established inn, giving its name to what is now usually called Dene-street, then Ram Alley.

Up Ram Alley was a very old-established chimney sweep, who kept a shop, or rather his wife kept it. The window dressing of this shop was not, perhaps, designed to attract customers in the way present-day window dressing is.

All that seemed to be sold in this shop in Ram Alley was saveloys, which have now disappeared, I think, from English markets. They could, at the time about which I am writing be purchased in Ram Alley for one penny each. The other articles sold and displayed were bundles of pimps, or lighting wood.

Over the door of the shop was a sign, suspended on a horizontal bar much in the way of the sign of a public house, and showing in colour a house in a street with one of the chimneys afire rather badly, and a couple of sweeps running to the scene of disaster.

The baker's shop in Ram Alley was as at present situated, but then kept by Mr. Borer.

Farther up near the entrance to Heath Hill, was a very dark and dirty chandler's shop kept by one Mr. Brown. He was mostly to be seen in his very broken-down low four-wheeled chaise, that had in its early days been used as a pleasure conveyance. Although built for that purpose, it was appropriated by Mr. Brown by a few slight additions to act as his commercial vehicle. It had once been painted a light blue.

Immediately opposite the bottom of Heath Hill, Mrs. Bartlett kept a small grocers and provision shop. The old houses have been demolished and new ones built on the site. Coming back to High-street, we pass the White Horse Hotel, and if we arrive at 2 o'clock in the afternoon we should notice a four-horse coach arrive, announcing its coming before

Dinnage's Recollections of Old Dorking

reaching the hotel by a bugle call.

The horses were soon taken to stables at the back of the premises, and a lively few minutes was taken up by the few passengers alighting and chatting.

The coach came from London, and was due to return at 3.30 pm the same day, and it was pleasant to witness the scene of the departure.

The fishmonger's shop was next to what was the Capital and Counties Bank opened by Dye & Theobald, and passed to Mr. Pilcher of the Mac Fisheries. The shop next to the "White Horse" was in the possession of Mr. Hickman, already referred to.

At the corner west of the way up to the Red Lion stables was then an establishment kept by Mr. Kendall as an upholsterers and furniture shop. He was also agent for sewing machines and sold carpets.

Owner of a large pantechnicon, he was in competition with Mr. John Chart, mentioned earlier, who also owned a pantechnicon, and undertook the removal of the furniture and chattels of people desiring to change houses, a desire more easily complied with than at the end of the year AD 1950!

There were two chemist's shops on the left-hand side of High-street going towards Pump Corner, and on the high pavement. One was kept by Mr. Clift - afterwards by Mr. Wilson, and now faded out - and the other, a very old-established business conducted by Mr. W.W. Clark. The frontage of this shop was very little altered from the appearance it presented to me as a youngster until recently, but now Messrs. Savory & Moore have put in a modern front.

The premises I have omitted to mention next to "The White Horse" going east, the gas offices, I ought to record as being the house occupied by Dr. Curtis, who for many years practised in Dorking. He owned certain property in the Station-road, then as now known as Spring-gardens and also land close by upon which was built later a number of cottages now known as Curtis-gardens. On the retirement of Dr. Curtis, the practice was taken

- 53 -

Dinnage's Recollections of Old Dorking

over by a Dr. Hopcroft, and later Dr. Batson.

Passing along the high path towards Pump Corner we come to the shop of Mr. Baxter, the pork butcher and sausage maker, and then the ironmongers kept by Messrs. Saubergue.

Mr. Joseph Mason was then called a cheesemonger, and the exterior of his shop going west is still as in his day. An example of the very old style of shop window, it gives a very pleasant effect to the part of High-street in which it is situated.

Next to the "Chequers Yard" was a shop that, as a boy, I could never pass without a long gaze at the window. It was the leading toy shop of the town kept by Miss Agate. All the choice toys of the day were to be seen, and inside was a perfect fairyland to youngsters. Huge rocking-horses, targets for archery, cricket bats, toy pop-guns, and toys of all descriptions were discernible in the recesses and background of the shop.

One used every device to get inside the shop to catch a fleeting sight of the delectable display.

Then came a corn shop kept by Messrs. J. & W. Attlee, now replaced by the Provincial Bank.

Dinnage's Recollections of Old Dorking

West Street

Passing over the road and with the Pump Corner to the left we continue our stroll down West-street (left side). Passing the entrance to Mr. Brown's bakery, we soon came to an old sweet shop kept by Mrs. Crompton. She sold some renowned confectionery known today as "Humbugs" - and good they were too.

West-street would not be West-street without mention being made of the chemist's shop which was situated next to, or quite near, Mrs. Crompton's, and kept by Mrs. White. This lady dealt in homeopathic medicines, and most of the people of the town were acquainted with "White the Homeopathic".

The business subsequently removed to High-street, close to, and on the east side of "The Ram".

A few shops, and then there was the butcher's shop kept by Mr. Dick Fuller, who sold good English meat, and without stint in those days. This gentleman served his town, as did his brother, Mr. Arthur Fuller, of South-street, before mentioned, in the Volunteer Fire Brigade.

Another well-known character of West-street was the owner of the good-class fish shop almost immediately opposite the "Bell Hotel", and part of which is now the Singer machine shop. This fish establishment was in the capable hands of Mr. Jack Rapley.

It was known by the public in his day that if anything was required in the fish, poultry or game line, from a pair of kippers to a pheasant or a turkey, they would get good stuff at Jack Rapley's. The shop had a bow type of window, and was entered by ascending two or three steps, the floor being higher than the pathway of West-street.

Mrs. Rapley, the good wife of Mr. Jack, kept at the back of the fish-shop a small stock of pottery of a very useful type, although not of the class generally understood by "Dresden" or "Worcester" and the like.

Dinnage's Recollections of Old Dorking

Mr. Bolland kept a greengrocer's and confectionery shop for a good many years (still the left side of West-street) opposite the iron railings of the Congregational Chapel. Then until the way leading to the yard of the builders, Messrs. Hanblin Bros. was constructed, the houses were all residential.

The next most notable establishment was that of the tea-taster and tea specialist, Mr. William Hollier. This gentleman occupied the premises for many years, as did his father before him. Mr. William Hollier delivered tea for many miles around Dorking, both in Surrey and Sussex, and Hollier's tea was a very well-known commodity.

Hollier's tea sold out for the last time a number of years ago, and the premises have greatly changed - a reminder that all things will come to an end.

Before finishing this imaginary walk in the Dorking of 80 years ago, I would like to say a few words about the Deepdene mansion. In the days before the construction of the by-pass in the 1930's a private coach road ran in front of the building and terminated at a gate just about opposite the field gate still in existence in Chart-lane.

In those days Chart-lane was the only public road into Dene-street and the town from this direction. On the left-hand side going into town is a meadow where I recollect in the late 1870s and 1880s the Summer Weeks of the Congregational Church Sunday School were held.

I attended on more than one occasion and remember we used to play the popular game of "Kiss in the Ring". The meadow was entered from the lower end through cart gates which stood on the site where houses now stand.

Just beyond was a horse pond, and when the circus came to Cotmandene horses and elephants paused here to drink. On the opposite side of Chart-lane was a bank of rhododendron which, in bloom, formed an exceedingly attractive display which drew sightseers from over a wide area.

This, then, was the Dorking I grew up in.

Index

Page-numbers in this Index are preceded by the letter R for Rose, A for Attlee and D for Dinnage, e.g. the first entry for Abel refers to page R80, meaning page 80 in the Rose booklet. The booklets are bound in the sequence of Rose, then Attlee, then Dinnage.

Abel, Mr, cricketer R80
Abel, John A4, A16
Academy, the R13
Acres, bakers, High St A5
Adams, gardener at Shrub Hill estate A4
Adams, Mr. shopkeeper, West St A13
Adams, Mr H A21
Adds, John A3
Adlard's Bartholomew Press A10, D32
Adsett, Mr A21
Agar, Miss, schoolmistress R59
Agate, Miss, toyshop D54
Alehouse, Mr. Lucock, High St A7
Aletaster R40-41
Alexander, Father D20
Alexander, a lady living adjacent to Independent Meeting House R52
Allatson, Mr, West St A13
Allen, Grant D29-30
Alloway, Mr, butcher, High St A5
Alloway, Mr, cyclist D48
Alloway, Charles A5
Alloway, George D48
Alloway, William A5
Almshouses, Cotmandene R29, R45
Althorp, Mr, reformer R108
Ambulance Corps A19
Anchor Yard R21
Andrews, Miss, schoolmistress R59
Andrews, Messrs, High St music warehouse A5

Andrews, West St music shop A12
Andrews and Court, musical instrument sellers D51
Annual Cattle Fair R71
Antiques:
  A W & W Eade Antiques Ai, A13
  Mid-Surrey Antiques A12
  Old House A13
  Pump Corner Antiques A8
  West St Antiques A14
Apostolic Catholic (Irvingite) Church R113
Archery Meetings R66
Architects, Frederick Muggeridge A9
Arnold, Matthew D30
Artist, Mr. Dawes D51
Arundel Rd R7
Ashworth, Mr, estate agent D47
Atkinson, Mr, West St A14
Attlee, Mrs, High St A8
Attlee, Edmund W A16
Attlee, Harriet Ai
Attlee, John Ri, Ai-ii, A1, A8
Attlee, Richard Ai-ii, A8, A16.
Attlee, William Ai
Attlee, Messrs J & W Aii, A8, D22, D54
Attree & Sons A5
Attwood, Mr, reformer R108
Auctioneers:
  High St R25
  William Miller A2
Avery, Rev G A19

Memories of Old Dorking

Back Fields R11
Back Lane see Church St (formerly Back Lane)
Bacon, Mr A20
Bailey Mrs, coach accident victim R77
Bakehouse, South St R35
Bakers:
  Acres, High St A5
  Mr. Beckett, South St A11
  Mr. Borer D52
  Mr. Brown D55
  John Brown A8
  High St R21, R25
  Mr. Jones D42
  Jonathan Pullen A5
  South St R2
  Mr Uwins R82
Balchin, Mr F A20
Balchin, Joseph A5
Balchin & Penn A5
Band of Hope D7
Bands R14, R89, R109, R114, A19, D45
Bandstand A12, D8
Banks:
  Barclays A2
  Capital and Counties A6
  East St R2
  High St R24-5
  London County and Westminster A7, A17
  Midland A12
  Nash and Neale's A6
  National Provincial A8
  Piper and Dewdney's A2
  private R66-8
Barbers:
  Mr Caffyn, High St A6, D43
  Harvey, High St A1
  High St R27, A8
  Kings Head (Anchor) Yard R21-2
  Mr Maber D35
  Jackie Mabie D47
  Mr Mills, High St A6
  Mr Murphy, West St A13
  Robert Spratley D43

Barbers (cont)
  Messrs Wickham & Son A8
  Mr. Wilson D43
Barclay family, Bury Hill Farm D24
Barclay, Mrs, widow of Robert Barclay R11
Barclay, Charles R10
Barclay, David R10
Barclay, Mr R A21
Barclay, Robert R10
Barclays Bank A2
Bargman, Mr, painter and decorator D12
Bargman & Sons, decorators & plumbers D41
Bargman, Messrs, South St A9
Barracks, the see Chapel Cottages
Barrington House (formerly The Orchard) R7
Barrington Rd D13
Bartholomew Press A10, D32
Bartlett, Mr, West St, blacksmith A13
Bartlett Mrs, grocer D52
Basket shop, Banks Farrand A2
Basketmakers A17
Batchelor, Mr, maltster A16
Batemans, High St A1
Batson, Dr D54
Batson, Mr, South St A11
Batson, W L A5
Baverstock, Mr, West St cooper A12-13
Baxter, Mr, butcher D54
Beadle R41
Beadle, Postman R3
Beckenham Rooms D3, D4
Beckett, Miss, schoolmistress R59
Beckett, Mr, South St, grocer and baker A11
Beckett, John R31-2, R46, A12

Index

Beckett, Mr W, tailor A8
Beecham Mr, workhouse master A10
Beecham Mr Jesse R34
Beggar-poker R41
Beggar's Opera, the R16
'Belgowan' D21
Bell, the (formerly the Star) R12, R15, R63, A6, A13, A15, D55
Bench Room R103
Benefit Club R62-3
Bents Brook D11
Bentworth Priors D2, D8, D12
Betchworth A16
Betchworth Borough R36
Betchworth Castle R9-10
Betchworth Park R66
Beves, Miss D47
Beves, Mr, clockmaker D47
Bill posting station, West St R14
Bingham, Mr, schoolmaster R58
Bird, Mrs, Clarendon House, West St A14
Bird, Elizabeth A14
Biscombe-Gardiner, Mr, artist D10
Bishop, Hugh R11
Black Horse, the R27, A3, D49
Blackburn, Miss Julia A7
Blacksmiths:
  Mr Bartlett, West St A13
  High St R28
  Horsham Rd R7
  London Rd/Reigate Rd R1
  West St R12, R16, A15
Blaker, Matthew A2
Blue Ribbon Army D6
Board of Guardians of the Poor D48
Bolland, Mr, greengrocer and confectioner D56
Bond, Mr, High St A6
Brookers, timber merchants D1

Bookshops:
  Dorking Bookshop A9
  Mr Hickman D35
  Websters Bookshop A9
Boorer, Mr G M, tobacconist A8
Boots see Shoes A6
Borer, Mr, baker D52
Borer, Mrs, newsagent D42
Bothwell, J R80
Bothwell, S R80
Bothwell, Samuel R31, A14, A16
Bottesford Charity R44
Botting, Mr D22-3
Botting, Richard A14
Bowring, Mr, brickmaker A17
Bowshell, James R40
Box, John, boarding school D50-51
Box Hill R33, R94-5, D7
Boxall, Mr, maltster A16
Boxall, Charles R82
Boxall's Brewery A2, A16, D45, D49
Boyce, Mr, workhouse governor R34
Brace, Mr, missioner D5, D6, D8
Bradley, John A12
Bradley Farm A15
Brandram, Mr A G A21
Bravery, James R35, A10, A16
Brayley, Mr, author of History of Surrey R46, R92, R96, R98
Brewer, Miss, schoolmistress R59
Breweries A16, D45-6
  Boxall's A2, A16, D45, D49
  James Cheesman A9
  High St R21, R27
  Mr Lucock, High St A7
  South St R32, R34
  West St R14
  John Young D39
Brewery House A9
Brian Cottage D29

Memories of Old Dorking

Brick yards A17
Brickhouse, West St R12
Bricklayers yard, South St R35
Bright, Rev J S D20
Briscoe, Mr, parliamentary candidate R100
Bristow, Mr A20
British School, Church St/Norfolk Rd see Powell Corderoy School (formerly British School); Royal British Schools
Broad, William (Old Hold Hard) R3, R23, R73-5, A8, A13
Brock, Curate D33
Brock, Dr D33
Brook, the R84
Brougham, Mr, reformer R108
Brown, Mr, baker D55
Brown, Mr, chandler D52
Brown, Mr, confectioner D45, D46
Brown, John A8
Buckland, Mr, watcher R107
Builders:
  Samuel Bothwell A14
  Mr Cole D5
  John Fell D5
  Mr Grinstead D5
  Hanblin Bros D56
  Job Pledge D3
  William Shearburn D32-33
  Edward Walker A10
  Mr White, High St A3
Builders yard, West St R15
Building Society, Nationwide A6
Bull Ring R20-21
Bull, John A11
Bull's Head Inn R2, R31, R70, R76, R77, A8, A17, A18, D42
Bunkers Hill D18, D19

Burden, Mary Ri
Burdett, Sir Francis R2
Burke, Mr (a burker) R110
Burrell, Mr A20
Bury Hill A10
Bury Hill Farm D24, D25
Burton, Montague A2
Bus Garage D30
Bus Station A11
Bush Inn D27
Butcher and Son's A15
Butchers R5
  John Adds A3
  Alloway, High St A5
  Mr Baxter D54
  Arthur Fuller D46
  Dick Fuller A13
  H Fuller A13
  J Fuller A13
  Joseph Fuller A10
  High St R26, A7, A8
  Mr Jenkins D36
  George King A14
  Mansons, High St A6
  Mr. Martyr, High St A8
  Niblett, High St A5
  Thomas Rose A15
  South St R2, R34
  F F Tracey D36
Butler, Mr A20
Butler, Mr, grocer D13, D44
Butler, Mr H A21
Butt, Mr G E P A21
Butter Hill R2, R32, R100, Di, D39

Cabinet maker and upholsterers, John Chart D48
Caffyn, Mr, High St barber A8, D43
Cage (or lock-up) R2, R34, A10
Callen, Mr, Bentworth Priors D8
Calvert, Mrs, Hill Crest D19
Calvinistic Meeting House R46, R54
Camelot, High St A5
Candle factories R13, R25, R27, A17

Index

Candle makers:
   William Cheesman A3
   Beetham Wilson A7
Cape Place R25, D48
Capital and Counties'
   Bank A6
Capon, Mr, woodman D19
Car Park A3
Carpenters:
   Mr Hazelgrove D41
   High St R28
   Edward Walker A10
Carriers:
   Tom Elms D38
   John Jeal D38
   James Razzell A14, A15
   West St R14, R16
Cartmen, Harry Knight D30
Castle Mill A16
Cat's Fields R7, D40
Cat's Fields Alley <u>see</u>
   Vincent's Walk
Ceaton, Mr and Mrs R58
Chabot, Alfred D25-26
Chalcraft, Mr, South St
   A10
Chalcraft, Arthur,
   florist and nurseryman
   D17
Chalcraft, Billy D17
Chaldecott, Mr H A21
Chaldecott, Mr W R61, A7
Chalk Pit R18, R30, R36
Chamberlain, John, crier
   R41, R112
Chandlers:
   Mr Brown D52
   Mrs Chatfield, High St
   A6
   <u>see also</u> Tallow
     chandlers
   Chapel Cottages (form-
     erly the Barracks)
     R19, R111
Chapels:
   West St R15
   <u>see also</u> Meeting
     Houses
Charles II, King of
   England R87
Charman, Mrs, dressmaker
   and milliner, High St
   A6

Charman, Jack A6
Chart, John, cabinet
   maker etc D48, D53
Chart Lane D56
Chart Park R10, R29
Chatfield, Mrs, chandler
   and greengrocer, High
   St A6
Cheesemongers, Joseph
   Mason D54
Cheesman, Mr, maltster
   A16
Cheesman, Mrs, High St
   A2
Cheesman, Mrs, formerly
   wine and spirit mer-
   chant A9
Cheesman, Mrs Harriott
   R20
Cheesman, James A9, A16
Cheesman, William A3
Cheesman and Bromley A8
Chemists:
   W W Clark D53
   Clarke, High St A7
   Mr Clift D53
   Mr Cousins, High St A2
   Mr Doubleday D35-6
   Mr Durrant D49
   Robert Best Ede A7, A17
   High St R3
   Paffard, High St A6
   Savory and Moore D53
   Mr Wilson D53
Chemists, homeopathic,
   Mrs White D55
Chequers R22
Chequer(s) Yard R22,
   R23-4, D54
Cherry Fair R71
Chevertons A3
Chichester, Mrs A21
Chichester, Rev E A A19
Chimney sweeps:
   Mr Dearling D13
   High St R29
Chinashops:
   Misses Randall D44
   Spratley, High St A2
   Robert Trimmer A2
Chipping Borough R36
Chislet Charity R44

Memories of Old Dorking

Chitty, Mr A20
Chitty, Mr, coachman R72-3
Chitty 'Neighbour' R12
Chitty, Richard R105, A15
Chopstick Place R33, D40, D41
Christmas Poultry Market R70
Church Passage (formerly Church Gates) R25
Church Pavement D49
Church St (formerly Back Lane) R6, R18, R19-20, R36, R38, R111, A10, A16, D33, D39
Churches:
  Apostolic Catholic R113
  Congregational R51, D7, D50, D56
  Methodist A10, D36
  North Holmwood R106, A17
  Parish Church R85, R90, A21, D1, D8
  Roman Catholic D20
  St Martha, Chilworth D10
  St Martin's R45-9, D1, D9, D26, D32
  St Paul's A19, D2, D8-9, D15
  Wesleyan R19, A11
  West St Chapel A13
  see also Friends Meeting House; Society of Friends; Presbyterians; United Reform Church
Churchill, Mr, musical instrument seller D47
Churchwardens R44
Cinema D39
Circus, at Cotmandene D56
Clapton, Richard A10
Clarendon House R12, A14

Clark, R T, printer, publisher and bookseller D48
Clark, W W, chemist D53
Clarke, chemist, High St A7
Cleaners Eastmans, South St A8
Cleere, John R49
Cleere, John Paul R19, R47
Clerk to the Magistrates R28
Clift, Mr, chemist D53
Cliftonville Estate D3, D14, D29
Clockmakers:
  Mr Beves D47
  Thomas Hubbard A2
  Thos Hubbard Jnr A7
  Samuel Reeves A14
Clothiers:
  Messrs R & W Marsh A8
  W A Marsh D46
  Tebb Bros D46
  West St A13
'Clovelly' D2
Coachbuilders:
  Messrs Sherlock A13
  High St R28
  Mr Walker, High St A4, D50
Coachmen:
  William Broad (Old Hold Hard) R3, R23, R73-5, A8, A13
  Mr Shaw R72
  Mr Walker R72
Coal Merchant, Jimmie Johnson D36-7
Coast Hill R106
Cobblers:
  Mr Robinson, West St A15
  Mr Slipper, West St A15
Cobden, Miss, schoolmistress A11
Cockchaffer Lane R33
Coldharbour Rd D21, D22
Cole, Mr, builder D5
Cole, Mr W A2

Index

Cole, W, leather cutter D48-9
Cole(s) & Adams, grocers A9, D45
Colgate, Mr (cricketer) R80
Colgate, Charles A7
Collins, Engineer D2
Colls & Sons A9-10
Coombe, Mr D A20
Coombes, Mr, cricketer R80
Combs, Mr, Red Lion A6
Confectioners:
    Mr Bolland D56
    Mr Brown D45, D46
    John Brown A8
    Butcher & Son's A15
    High St R21
    John Hubbard A9
    Mr Loyns D45, D46
    Jonathan Pullen A5
    Mr Rix D45
    Richard Uwins A7
    Messrs Wickham & Son A8
    Mr Wickham D45
Congregational Church D7, D50, D56
Congregational Meeting House R51
Convent School, Harrow Rd D20
Cook's shop, West St A13
Cooke, Phillip R41, A3
Cooper, Misses, District Visitors D15-16, D19
Co-op A12, D39
Coopers A17
    Mr Baverstock, West St A12-13
    Banks Farrand A2
Corderoy, Miss, Benefactor of British School D11-12
Corn dealers:
    John Charman A6
    James Wells A9
Corn Market R26, R69
Corn merchants, Messrs J & W Attlee A8, D22, D54
Cornish, Dr, Old House, South St A10
Cotmandene (formerly the Heath) R6, R29, R30, R71, R80, R88, R107, R108, R109, D51, D56
Cottage Hospital D29
Cottagers Show R65-6
Cotton, Sir Arthur D2-3, D12
Cotton, Lady D2
Cotton, Miss see Hope, Lady
Council Offices A9
County Hospital D29
Court Baron R38, R48
Court Leet R38, R41, R48
Court of the Manor of Dorking R38
Cousin, Mr, headmaster of British School D11
Cousins, Mr, chemist A2
Cranford, William A4
Crawford, R W R10
Crawford, William R10, R104
Cricketers, the R34-5, A11, D43
Crier Chamberlain R41, R112
Crockery, Spratley, High St A2
Crompton, Mrs, sweetshop D55
Cromwell, Oliver R87
Croucher, Mrs, schoolmistress D34
Croucher, Mr, greengrocer D35
Croucher, Nehemiah D34-5
Croucher, Messrs, greengrocers A9
Cubitt, Thomas R9
Cullen, W, West St offices A15
Curn, Edith A21
Curry, Mr, harness-maker, High St A2

Memories of Old Dorking

Curtain, Mr A20
Curtis, Dr D53
Curtis, George A5
Curtis, John Adee A9
Curtis, Thomas R72
Curtis Gardens D53

Dale, Mr, gardener, West St A14
Dame schools R58
  Church St D33, D34
  Mrs Gilliam A4
  Mrs Pethybridge A6
Daniels, Mr, Queen's Head A11
Darking R15
Davey, Frank D50
Davey, Messrs, High St A3
Davy, Mr, fishmonger, High St A5
Davy, Mrs (Aunt Hetty) A5
Davis, Mr, Tower House D8-9
Dawes, Mr, artist D51
Dawes, Mr, musical instrument seller D51
Dawes, Emery D36
Dawson, Rev Alfred R53
Dearling, Mr, chimney sweep D13
Decorators:
  Bargman & sons D41
  see also Painters (and decorators)
Deepdene, the R9, A9
Deepdene Car Centre A4
Deepdene coach road R8
Deepdene Estate R10
Deepdene Gardens R10, R29
Deepdene Lodge R8
Deepdene Mansion D56
Degenhardt, Charles Ri-ii, D45
Degenhardt's A9
Denbies R8-9, R99, R105
Dendy, Mr, builder of houses in South St A11
Dendy, Arthur A12

Dene, the see Cotmandene
Dene Hill R109
Dene St (formerly Ram Alley)R6, R28, R29, D52, D56
'Denfield' D1
Denison, Mr father of William Joseph Denison R9
Denison, William Joseph R8-9, R45, R99-101
Denison's Hill R9
Denison's New Road R105
Denny, Mr, second husband of Lady Hope D7
Dentist, Mr Durant D49
Devonshire, Duke of R93, R94
Dewdney, Mr, banker R67
Dewdney, Mrs, High St A3
Dewdney, Arthur D34, D35
Dewdney, George A2, A16
Dewdney, James A16
Dewdney, Robert A7
Dickens, Charles R74-6, A12
Dinnage, Henry Di
Dinnage, Mary Sarah (née Williams) Di
Dinnage, Rana Di
Dinnage, William Henry Di
Ditchling Singers R89
Dixon, Mr (late Doubleday), High St A6
Doctors:
  Batson D54
  Brock D33
  W Chaldecott A7
  Curtis D53
  William Hart A4
  Hopcoft D54
  Thomas Napper A6
  see also Surgeons
Donald & Westland, nurserymen R1
Donaldson, P C R112
Dorking, origin of name R15

Index

Dorking Advertiser Ai, A9, Di, D40
Dorking Agricultural Association R66
Dorking Band R14, R109, R114
Dorking Bank R67, R68
Dorking Bookshop A9
Dorking Cemetery D48
Dorking Christmas Poultry Show R66
Dorking Floors A15
Dorking Foundry A12
Dorking Mechanics Institute R28, R61-2
Dorking Museum A12
Dorking Patrol R95
Dorking Parish Church see Parish Church
Dorking Town Band R89
Dorking Tyre Service A9
Dorking Waterworks R19, D2
Dorking Yeomanry Cavalry Corps R2
Doubleday, Mr see Dixon, Mr (late Doubleday)
Doubleday, Mr, chemist D35-36
Down, Mrs, 'Elmhurst' D10
Down, Dondas D10
Down, Frank D10
Down, William D10
Down, Scott and Down, solicitors D10
Down's, Messrs A5
Drapers:
  Misses Julia Blackburn and Jane Puzey A7
  Charles Degenhardt D45
  Fielder Bros D46
  High St R24
  William Latter A7
  Mr Newitt Ri
  Nicklin & Co A3
  I R Overton A6
  Charles Rose Ri-ii, D45
  West St R16, A12

Drawbridge, Mr, cricketer R80
Dressmakers:
  Misses Adam, High St A4
  Mrs Charman, High St A6
  Miss Gittins, High St A8
  Mrs Tooley, South St A12
Duke's Head, Bear Green R23
Duncumb, Misses, South St A11
Dunns, furriers, High St A4
Durant, Mr, chemist and dentist D49
Durham, Mr, reformer R108
Durrant, Mr A20, A21
Dutch House R26, R27
Dyas, Robert, ironmongers A7
Dye & Theobald, fishmongers D53
Dyers, High St A6

Eade (A W & W) Antiques Ai, A13
East Borough R36
East St R1-2, R61
Eastmans, cleaners, South St A8
Ebenezer Cottages R111
Ede, Robert Best A7, A11, A17
'Edgecombe' D14
Edwards, Jonathan A9
Eives, Miss, schoolmistress R59
Eives, George A7
'Elmhurst' D10
Elms, Tom D38
Employment agencies, Sirrons A8
Entertainers:
  Jack Greathurst D42
  I C U Minstrels A20, D42-3, D45
  Walter Whaley D42

Memories of Old Dorking

Estate agents:
  Mr Ashworth D47
  High St R25
  White and Sons D17, D49
    (formerly Alexander & Archibald White)
Etam A3
Evans, Miss, schoolmistress R58
Evening Star D45

Fairbrother, Mr, Goodwyns Farm D11
Falkland Hill (formerly Bunkers Hill) D18
Falkland Rd R7, R111, A11, D3, D13, D18, D27, D37
Falkland School D49
'Falklands, the' D16
Farley, Mrs, West St laundry A13
Farm Lane D24
Farmer George R16
Farrand, Banks A2
Feachem, Rev George R35, R49, D32
Fell, John D5
Fellmonger, Matthew Blaker A2
'Fernside' D15
Field, Mr 'Southease House' D21
Fielder Bros, drapers D46
Fife and Drum Band D45
Finch, Richard, 'Lord Finch' R3, A12
Fire Brigade A19, D44, D48, D55
Fire Station A14, D4
Fishmongers:
  Davy, High St A5
  Dye & Theobald D53
  High St R27
  Lovell, High St A1
  Mr Pilcher (Mac Fisheries) D53
  Jack Rapley D55
  Mr Tugwell D44
Flint Hill A17, D11

Flood, Curate D1
Flood, Misses, 'Denfield' D1
Florists and nurserymen:
  Arthur Chalcraft D17
  Harry Lucas D17, D33
Floyd, F W, grocer D47
Fly proprietors:
  Emery Dawes D36
    see also Horses and carriages; Horse buses
Ford, Mr, market gardener D38
Fordland Charity R44-5
Foreman, Mr, owner of Pipp Brook Mansion R10
Forresters' R62, A19
Fosterwoods Meadow R8
Foundries, Dorking
Foundry A12
Fowl market see Poultry Market
Fox, the R105
Fox fair R71
Franklin, Mr, furnisher and upholsterer D46
Freeman, Hardy & Willis A7
Friary & Holroyd A13
Friary Offices A13
Friendly Society R62
Friends Meeting House R15, R16, R46, R50-51, A13, Di, D39
Fuller, Misses, High St A3-4
Fuller, Mr D35
Fuller, Mr, brickmaker A17
Fuller, Mrs, South St A11
Fuller, Arthur, butcher D46, D55
Fuller, Dick, butcher D55
Fuller, Mr H A13
Fuller, John A13, A14
Fuller, Joseph A10
Fuller, Richard R73-4
Fuller, Sydney A20

Index

Fuller, Mr W S A21
Fuller, S & Son A7
Fullers Field D35-6
Furnishers:
   Frank Davey D50
   Mr Franklin D46
Furniture warehouse:
   William Miller A2
   Joseph Sayers A13
Furriers, Dunns, High St A4

Gale, Mr, banker R67
Garages, Mays Garage A11
Gardeners:
   Mr Dale, West St A14
   Mr Stringer D17
   Mr Priest D19
Garth, the, nursing Home D3
Gas Company Aii, A7
General shops:
   Mrs Gittins, High St A5
   Mr Mitchell, High St A5
George IV, King of England R108
Gibbet, Sandy Cross D22
Giles Green gravelpit R43
Gilliam, Miss (Mrs Lanham) schoolmistress R59
Gilliam, Mr A20
Gilliam, Mr, stonemason, High St A4
Gilliam & Son's, statuary showroom A15
Girlin, Mr, sewing machine agent D41
Gittins, Mr, whitesmith A5
Gittins, Mrs, dressmaker, High St A8
Gittins, Mrs, general store, High St A5
Glass shop, Robert Trimmer A2
Glaziers, John Fuller & Richard Botting A14
Glenda Gray A4

Glory Woods D14
Goble, Mrs, Hampstead Rd D28
Goble, Mr, pie man D28
Goddard, John A6
'Golden Canister' grocers R24, D47
Good Templar's R62, A19
Gooding, Mr D5
'Goodwyns' formerly 'Oakridge' D9, D11
Goodwyns Farm D11
Gorge Restaurant A7
Grammar School R28
Grantham, Rev Tom R D17
Graves, Mr, Red Lion Hotel A20
Great Reform Dinner R107
Greathurst, Miss, Spotted Dog D42-3
Greathurst, Mr A20
Greathurst, Jack, entertainer D42-3
Greaves, Mr, miller and agriculturist R12
Greaves, Richard A15
Greengrocers:
   Mr Bolland D56
   Mrs Chatfield, High St A6
   Mr Croucher D35
   Messrs Croucher A9
   Thomas Howard A9
   John Kennis A1
Grey, Mr, reformer R108
Griffin, Francis A1
Grinstead, Mr, builder D5
Grocers R5
   John Adds A3
   Mr Bartlett D52
   Mr Beckett, South St A11
   Mr Butler D13, D44
   Butter Hill R2
   Chequer(s) Yard R23
   Cole(s) & Adams A9, D45
   F W Floyd D47
   'Golden Canister', High St R24, D47
   James King A1

Memories of Old Dorking

Grocers (cont)
  Messrs Kingham's,
    High St A2, D48
  John Norman A9
  W Norman R86
  Robert Pearce D47, D48
  Mr Philpot, High St
    A1-2
  Mr Plant D13
  Mr Portsmouth D45
  George Robinson A5
  Thomas Rose A15
  Mr Sayers, South St
    A10
  South St R2
  Edward Warley A7
  West St R15
  Mr White, High St A5
  Thomas Wood D48
Grout, Mr, centenarian
  R109
Grove House R12
Guildford Co-operative
  Society D39
  see also Co-op
Gumbrell, Misses, milliners, Pump Corner
  A8
Gurney, Joseph John R50-51

Hairdressers, Jerome D46
Hall, Mrs, 'Bentworth
  Priors' D8
Hall, Martha R15
Hall, William R15
Hamblin, George (Fox)
  R84
Hamblin, Henry (Chick)
  R84
Hamblin, John (Sailor
  Jack) R84
Hanblin Bros, builders
  D56
Hampshire Banking Co
  R27
Hampstead Lane School
  R10
Hampstead Rd R7, Di,
  D14, D18, D28, D29,
  D37
Harbroe, Thomas A10

Harding, Mr, Queen's
  Head, jobmaster D27,
  D32
Hare, Mr (a burker) R111
Harmer's Autos A10
Harrow Gate Gardens D2
Harrow Lodge D13
Harrow Rd D12, D19
Harrow Rd East R7, D1,
  D12, D13, D28
Harrow Rd West D10-21,
  D28
Harrow Toll Gate R7
Harrowgate Estate D3
Harness-maker:
  Mr Curry, High St A2
  George Dewdney A2
  Jonathan Edwards A9
  Mrs Smith, West St
    A13
Hart, Alexander A104
Hart, Charles R66
Hart, John R28
Hart, Thomas R28
Hart, William A4
Hart & Sons, solicitors
  A5
Hart, Messrs R72
Hart, Scales & Hodges
  (formerly Hart & Martin) A3, D16
Hart Rd D50
Harvey, Mr, barber A1
Hatter, Robert Dewdney
  A7
Haybarn House A10
Headboroughs R38
Heath, the see Cotmandene
Heath Hill D52
Hendon, Mr, aeronaut D35
Heselgrove, Mr, carpenter and joiner D41
Hickman, Mr, bookseller
  D35, D53
Hicks, 'Crazy' R114-15
Hicks, Mr, linen draper
  Ri
Hicks, Richard A3
Higglers A17
High Constable R38

Index

High School (formerly
  Parsonage House) A15
High St R3, R6, R20-29,
  R36, R67, R82, R99,
  R112, Ai, A16, A20,
  Di, D17, D22, D47-54
  North A1-4
  South A4-8
Highwaymen R20
'Hill Crest' D19
'Hill View' D20
Hoad, Charlie, 'the
  moonlight baker' D32
Holden, Matthew R72,
  R76, A3
Holder House R33, A12,
  D23, D38, D39
Hole-in-the-Wall R33,
  R93, R94
Hollier, William D56
Hollow, the R7
Hollow Hill R7
Holloway farmhouse R7
Holly & Laurel R64
Holmwood Borough R36
Holmwood Common R107,
  D11
Holmwood Common Committee Aii
Holmwood Windmill R46
Hooker & Nicholls A2
Hopcroft, Dr D54
Hope, Henry Thomas R9
Hope, Admiral Sir James
  D2
Hope, Lady D2, D3, D4-5,
  D7-8, D39
Hope, Thomas R9
Horse bus drivers:
  Mr King D36
  Mr Swift D36
Horse buses D36
Horses and carriages D3
Horsham Rd R7, A20, D1,
  D5, D25, D29, D30-31
Horsham Turnpike D3,
  D12
Horsham Turnpike Rd D26,
  D28
Horticultural Society
  R65-6

Hospitals:
  cottage Aii, D29
  county D29
Hotels:
  Temperance Hotel A114
  see also Public
  houses
House of Flowers A4
Howard, Mr, veterinary
  surgeon A3
Howard, Thomas A9
Howard Rd R7, A14
Hoxton Hall D6
Hubbard, Mr, 'Woodcote'
  D3
Hubbard, James D48
Hubbard, John A9
Hubbard, Thomas A2
Hubbard, Thos Jnr A7
Hudson, Mr A20
Hudson, M F A21
Hughes, Rev Geoffrey D1
Hull, Mr, Surrey Yeoman
  A5
Humphrey, T R81
Hunt, Mr, reformer R108
Hutchins, Mr, miller,
  Holmwood A16
Hutton, Eleanor A13

I C U Minstrels A20,
  D42-43, D45
Imperial Club A3
Independent Meeting
  House R46, R51-4
International Stores A3
Iron foundry, West St
  R14
Ironmongers:
  William Dean A2
  High St R25
  Charles Peirson D42
  Peirson & Co A2
  W J Rossiter D42
  Saubergue, Messrs D54
  Stone & Turner A7
Isard, Miss, toy shop,
  High St A7
Ison, Mr, relieving
  officer D42-3
Ison, Mr W A20

Memories of Old Dorking

Ivery, Mr, nursery gardener D50
Ivery & Son A4
'Ivy Holt' D50

Jeal, John D38
Jeal, William D11
Jenkins, Mr, butcher D36
Jerome, hairdresser D46
Jewellers:
  High St R25
  James Hubbard D48
Jobmasters:
  Mat Napper D27
  Mr Harding D27
Johnson, Mr D38
Johnson, Mrs, confectioner D36-7
Johnson, Jimmie D36-7
Jolliffe, Mr, parliamentary candidate R100
Jolly Brewers R26
Jones, Mr, baker and confectioner D42
Jones, Mr T A20
Joyce, Mr, tailor D45
Joyce, Rev James R49
Junction Rd R14, R33, A9, A14, D5, D12, D39, D41
Jupp, H R80, R81
Justices Room R104

Kendall, Mr, furnisher and upholsterer D53
Kennis, 'Betty' A1
Kennis, John A1
Kentucky Fried Chicken A4
King, Mr, horse bus driver D36
King, Mr, maltster, High St A1
King, George A14
King, James A1
Kingham, H G, offices, West St A15
Kingham & Co, wine and spirit store A7
Kinghams A1

Kingham's grocers A2, D49
King's Arms R15, R18, R21, R22, R75, A15
King's Head Square R18
King's Head Yard R21
King's Head R18, R21, R22, R75, D47
Knight, Harry D30
Knoll Rd A20, D3, D12, D25, D26

Labelliere, Major Peter R32, R33, R92-8
Ladies Seminaries R59
Lambert, Superintendent D40
Lamplighter, Mr Wicks R6
Landsell, Mr, schoolmaster R59-60
Langton, Charles R40
Lanham, Miss, postmistress D47
Lanham, Mrs (née Gilliam) R59
Lanham, H R21
Lanham, Henry R49, R60
Lanhams A1
Lascelles A4
Lascelles, Tickner & Co A4
Latter, William A7
Laundry, Mrs Farley, West St A13
Leather cutters, W Cole D48-9
Leatherhead Fair R72
Lecture Hall, Band of Hope D7
Lee, Mr T A20
Lee, Fred D40
Leech, Mr, parliamentary candidate R100
Leslie, Lady Elizabeth Jane see Wathen, Lady Elizabeth Jane
Leslie, Lady Mary A10
Leslie Rd, Pixham D18
Letts, Mr A A20, A21
Limeworks A16, D8
Lindsay, Joseph A13

Index

Literary and Scientific Institute R61
Little Chequers, the R28
Little Dudley House Restaurant A11
Lock-up see Cage
London coach D52-3
London Rd R1, R6, R8, R36, A4, D50
London Rd Mill R1
London and County Bank R24, R68
London County and Westminster Bank A7, A17
Long, Mr, parliamentary candidate R100-101
Longstock Charity R44
Lonsdale House D50
Louis Phillipe, King of France R11, A12
Lovell, fishmonger A1
Lovibonds A4
Lowndes, Mr, Rose Hill House A12
Lowndes, Richard R11
Loyns, Mr, confectioner D45, D46
Loyns, Pump Corner A8
Lucas, Harry, florist & nurseryman D17, D33
Lucock, Mr, alehouse and brewery, High St A7
Lucock, Mr, maltster A16
Lucock's Brewery D45, D46
Lynn, Mr, High St A6
Lynn, Mr, West St A13

Maber, Miss Una D35
Mabie, Jackie D47
MacDonald, George D30
Mac Fisheries D53
Mackney & Pierce A2
Mad Hatter D32
Maltings/maltsters/malthouses A16
  High St R24
  Mr King, High St A1
  North St R18

Maltings/maltsters/malthouses (cont)
  Mr Rudge, South St A11
Mansons, butchers, High St A6
Marine stores, Richard Skilton A9
Market gardeners:
  Mr. Ford D38
  Alec Robinson D13
  South St R35
Market House R18, R26, R35-6
Market Place R70
Marquis of Granby (Pickwick Papers) R74-6
Marsden, Mr A20
Marsh, Mr A20
Marsh, W A, clothier D46
Marsh, Messrs R & W A8
Marshall, Miss, 'Cliftonville' D11
Marshall, Mr, boot and shoeshop, High St A6
Martin, Mr, solicitor, High St A6, D16
Martin, a wool thief R112
Martineau, Mr, 'Goodwyns' D11
Martyr, Mr, butcher, High St A8
Mason, Mr A20
Mason, Mr, shopkeeper, High St A7
Mason, Rev John D40
Mason, Joseph, cheesemonger D54
Masons yard, West St R12
Mathews, Mr A20
Matthews, Mr G S A21
May-pole R86
Maybank, John R67
Maybank, Joseph D47-8
Mays Garage A11, D17, D32
Mechanics Institute R28, R61-2

Memories of Old Dorking

Methodist Church A10, D36
   see also Wesleyan Church
Medical Hall R21
"Meeting" see Independent Meeting House
Meeting House R50-54
   West St R15
   see also Friends Meeting House
Merryandrews R30
Mickleham A17
Mid-Surrey Antiques A12
Midland Bank A12
Miles, Mr E A21
Militia Club R110
Mill Lane R6, A2, A3, D45, D49
Miller, Mr A20
Miller, Mr H E A21
Miller, William A2
Millers:
   Messrs J & W Attlee A8, D22
   Elizabeth Bird A14
   Mr Hutchings, Holmwood A16
   Mill St (formerly Mill Lane) R27
Milliners:
   Misses Adams, High St A4
   Balchin & Penn A5
   Mrs Charman, High St A6
   Misses Gumbrell, Pump Corner A8
Mills, Mr, barber, High St A6
Mills, Mr, White Lion D45
Mills, Mrs, King's Arms A15
Mills:
   London Rd R1
   Milton Court A16
   Parsonage A15, A16, D22
   Pippbrook A4, A16
   Pixham A16
   Rookery A14, A16

Mills (cont)
   Westcott A10, A16
Milton Court Farm A16
Milton Court Mill A16
Milton St D24
Mission Hall, Junction Rd and West St D5
Missioners:
   Mr Brace D5, D6, D8
   J Ogram Webb D6, D8
Mister Fegan's Homes for Boys D8
Mitchell, Miss, schoolmistress A11
Mitchell, Mr, general shop, High St A5
Mole, the R96
Moleside, Pixham D18
Moonlight Baker, the (Charlie Hoad) D32
Moore, Joseph R29, A4
Moore, William R19
Moore & Weller, shopkeepers, West St A14
'Moore's Lane' R29
Moores Road D50
Moorhouse, Mr, High St A3
Moorhouse, Mr, photographer D50
Moorhouse, Henry D41
Morgan & Scott, publishers D5
Muffin and crumpet vendor, Woodger R5
Muggeridge, Frederick A9
Murphy, Mr, baker, West St A13
Museum A12
Mutual Improvement Society R62
Music shops:
   Andrews, West St A12
   Tarlings A13
   Mr Uwins Jnr, High St A7
Music warehouse, Andrews, High St A5

Index

Musical instrument
  sellers:
    Andrews & Court D51
    Mr Churchill D47
    Mr Dawes D51
Myrtle House D39
Myrtle Road D39

Nag's Head R106
Napper, Mat, jobmaster D27
Napper, Thomas A6
Nash, Mr, banker R67
Nash & Neale's Bank A6
National Provincial Bank A8
National Schools in the Mint R58
Nationwide Building Society A6
Neale, Mr, banker R67
Neale, Neddie D24
Neale's Farm see Bury Hill Farm
New Road D41
New Friendly Society R65
Newitt, Mr, linen draper R1
Newland, Mr, Rose Hill House A12
'Newra' D22
Newsagents:
    Mrs Borer D42
    Miss Spratley, South St A12
Niblett, Mr, butcher, High St A5
Niblett, John A2
Nicklin & Co, drapers A3
Noble, William D6
Nook, the D30
Norfolk, Duke of R35, R103, A5
Norfolk Arms R64, R106
Norfolk Rd D10, D38
Norman, John A9
Norman, W R86
North Holmwood Church R106, A17
North St R18-19, D47

Nower Rd D38
Nower, the A20, D21-2, D25
Nurserymen:
    Donald & Westland R1
    Mr Ivery D50
    Junction Rd R33
    Harry Lucas D17, D33
    South St A10
    Robert Westland, High St A4

'Oakhurst' D9
'Oakridge' D10, D11
Ockley Club R64
Oddfellows R62, A19
Old Hold Hard see Broad, William
Old House A10, D33
Old House, antiques A13
Old House at Home R14, A14
Old King's Head R18
Old Market House R88
Old Vicarage, South St D32
Olivier, Rev G K D9
Olivier, Sir Laurence D9
Orchard, the see Barrington House R7
Orchard House D28
Orchard Rd D28, D29, D37
Organists:
    E J R Russell R49, A6
    Miss N Todman D6
Outfitters, Messrs R & W Marsh A8
  see also Clothiers
Overseers R43, R44
Overton, Mr I R A6

P D S A A12
Paffard, Mr, chemist, High St A6
Painters (and decorators):
    Mr Bargman D12
    John Fuller and Richard Botting A14
    West St R13
Palladine, R, tailor, South St A8

Memories of Old Dorking

Palmer, Mr, parliamentary candidate R99
Palmer, William Isaac D6
Parfitt, F, & Son A8
Parish Church R85, R90, A21, D1, D8
<u>Parish Constable</u> R38
Park Farm R29
Parsonage Farm A15
Parsonage House (formerly The Parsonage, latterly High School) R12, A15
Parsonage Mill A15, A16, D22
Patching, Mr and Mrs R58
Pavilion D38
Paxon, Dr, 'Penny Readings' D40-41
Paygate D28
 see also Toll bars/gates: Turnpikes
Penn, William R27, A6
Pearce, Robert D47, D48
Peirson, Chas, ironmonger A2, D42
'Penny Readings' D40-41
Perceval, Mr, parliamentary candidate R100-101
Percival, W (Pess) R80
<u>Perfumer</u>, Robert Best Ede A7, A17
Peters, Mr A20
Peters, G (Ringer Peters) R80
Peters, Henry R9, R95
Peters, Messrs George & Son A8
Pethybridge, Mrs and Misses, dames school, High St A6
<u>Petty Constable</u> R38
Philpot, Mr, grocer A1
Philpott, R F D20
Philps, John A1, A3
Philps, Thomas A1
<u>Photographers</u>:
 Mr Moorhouse D50
 Mr Usherwood D49-50

<u>Pickwick Papers</u> R74-6, A12
Pieman, Mr Goble D28
Pigburn, Fanny R110-11
Pilcher, Mrs, fishmonger D53
Pine Cottage D20
Piper, Gale, Nash & Neale (Reigate, Croydon & Darking Bank) R67
Piper & Dewdney (Dorking Bank) R67, A2
Pipp Brook (The Washway) R13, A4, A16
Pipp Brook House Lodge R8
Pipp Brook Mansion R10
Pippbrook Mill A4, A16
Pithard, Mr, Headmaster of St Paul's D34
Pitt, Mr, High St A7
Pixham D18
Pixham Mill A16
Plant, Mr, grocer D13
Plat, the D39
Playfoot, Mr, High St R67
Pleasure Fair R32
Pledge, Fred D14
Pledge, Job D3
Pledge, Len D14
<u>Plumbers</u>:
 John Fuller and Richard Botting A14
 West St R13
Pneumatic Tent Co D35
<u>Police</u> R112
Police Station R32, R34, D40
<u>Police News</u> D44
Poole's Diorama D43
Portsmouth, Mr, grocer D45
Post Office R6, R21, R70, R71, A1, A3, A7, A9, A12, A17, D47
Post Office Corner R44
<u>Postmen</u>, Beadle R3
Potter, 'Host', The Bell Inn R15, A13

Index

Pottery sellers:
  North Holmwood A17
  Mrs Rapley D55
Poultry Market R70,
  A17-18
Pound, the R2, R32
Powell, Mr, benefactor
  of British School
  D10-11
Powell Corderoy School
  (formerly British
  School) D10, D11,
  D33, D34, D50
    see also Royal
  British Schools
Powis, Mr, assistant
  to Robert Best Ede
  A11
Presbyterians R51-2
Priest, Mr, gardener
  D19
Prince of Wales, public
  house R107, D28
Printers:
  R T Clark D48
  Robert Best Ede A7,
    A17
  Charles Rowe D43-4
  Mr Simmonds D47
  Tanners A9
  W H Smith & Sons D48
Priory Bungalow D2
Provident Institution
  R62
Provincial Bank D54
Public Hall, West St
  R13, D4
Public houses (including Hotels and Inns):
  The Bell Inn (formerly The Star) R12,
    R15-16, R63, A6,
    A13, A15, D55
  The Black Horse R27,
    A3, D49
  Bull's Head Inn R2,
    R31, R70, R76, R77,
    A8, A17, A18, D42
  Bush Inn D27
  Chequers R22
  Cricketers R34-5,
    A71, D43

Public houses (including Hotels and Inns)
  (cont)
  Duke's Head, Bear
    Green R23
  Fox R105
  Jolly Brewers R26
  King's Arms R15,
    A15
  King's Head R18,
    R21, R22, R75, D47
  Little Chequers R28
  Nag's Head R106
  Norfolk Arms R64,
    R106
  Old King's Head R18
  Prince of Wales D28
  Queen's Arms R16-
    18, R22, R61, A12
  Queen's Head Inn R2,
    R7, R35, R63, A71,
    D27, D32
  Ram Inn R28, R63,
    R71, A5, D52, D55
  Red Lion Hotel R3,
    R25, R38, R71, R77,
    R99, R102, R103,
    A6, A20, A21, D40,
    D53
  The Rock D46
  Rose and Crown R15-
    18
  Spotted Dog R32, A9,
    D42
  Star see Bell Inn
    (formerly the Star)
  The Sun A2-3, D49
  Surrey Yeoman Inn
    R28, R63, R71, A5,
    D50, D51
  Three Tuns Inn R26,
    R77, A3, D36, D49
  Wheatsheaf Inn R6,
    R24, R112, A1, A3
  White Hart Inn R28,
    R76
  White Horse Hotel
    R4, R101, A5-6,
    D52, D53

Memories of Old Dorking

Public houses (including Hotels and Inns) (cont)
  White Lion R30, A8, D45
  Windmill Inn D11
    see also Temperance Hotel
Pullen, Jonathan A5
Pump, the R20-21
Pump Corner A8, D45, D53, D54, D55
Pump Corner Antiques A8
Punch Bowl R8, R103, D17
Punch Bowl Fair R71
Puttock, Miss, St Margaret's, South St A10
Puzey, Miss Jane A7

Quakers see Society of Friends
Queen's Arms A12
Queen's Head Club R63-4
Queen's Head Inn R2, R7, R35, R63, A11, D27

Railway stations:
  L B & S C R (the Brighton Station) D21
  S E & C D10
  South Eastern R11, A15, D36
Ram Alley see Dene St
Ram Club R63-4
Ram Inn R28, R63, R71, A5, D52, D55
Randall, Misses, china shop D44
Ranmore Common R71, D30
Rapley, Jack D55
Rapley, Mrs, pottery seller D55
Rat-catcher R26-7
Rate collectors, George Alloway D48
Rayne, Mr, West St A13
Razzell, James A14, A15, R80
Rectory, North St R18-19
Red Lane R107

Red Lion Hotel R3, R25-6, R38, R71, R77, R99, R102, R103, A6, A20, A21, D40, D53
Redland Woods D11, D25
Redlands R107
Reeve, Miss, schoolmistress D38
Reeves, Mr, Headmaster of British School D34
Reeves, Mr, High St A5
Reeves, Samuel A14
Registrar of Births, Marriages and Deaths A11
Reigate Bank R67
Reigate, Croydon & Darking Bank R67
Reigate Rd R1, R8
Removals, John Chart D53
Rennies Direct London & Brighton Line R115
Restaurants:
  Gorge Restaurant A7
  Little Dudley House Restaurant A11
Reynolds A9
'Ribblesdale' D5
Ridgeway Rd D3, D22, D25
Rifle Volunteers A19
Rix, Mr, confectioner D45
Rix, Mr T G A21
Robins, High St A5
Robinson, Mr, cobbler, High St A15
Robinson, Alec, market gardener D13
Robinson, George A5
Rock Brewery D46
Rock, the, public house D46
Roman Catholic Church, Falkland Grove D20
Roman Rd D3, D12
'Rooftree' D12
Rookery, the R74
Rookery Mill, Westcott A14, A16
Roomes, Mr, shoemaker R111
Rose, Mr A20
Rose, Annie Tranter Ri

Index

Rose, Charles, draper Ri-ii, D45
Rose, 'Duckey' A20
Rose, Joshua A16
Rose, Richard A5
Rose, Thomas Ri, R14, R109, A15
Rose Cottage D14
Rose & Crown R15
Rose Hill R6-7, R51, A11
Rose Hill House A12
Rose Hill (Mansion) R11
Roses Cottages D40
Rossiter, Mr, High St R67
Rossiter, W J, ironmonger D42
Rothes, Countess of R10, R114, A4
Rothes, Earl of R10, A4, D51
Rothes Rd D50
Rotunda R31, R86, D13, D14
Rowe, Charles D43-4
Royal British Schools R58
  see also Powell Corderoy School
Rudge, John A11
Rudge, William A13
Russell, Mr, reformer R108
Russell, E J R, organist R49, A6
Ryde, Mr, South St A10

Sainsburys A7
St Margaret's, South St A10
St Martin's Church R45-9, D1, D9, D26, D32
St Paul's Church A19, D2, D8-9, D15
St Paul's Road (formerly Sweetheart's Lane) R7, D28, D31
St Paul's School D34
Sally, barbers wife R21-2
Salvation Army D3
Sanctuary R51
Sand Place see Sondes Place
Sandes, John A6
Sandy Cross D22, D25
Sandy Cross Lane R7
Sanford, Jack, Town Crier D36
Saubergue, P L A7
Saubergue, Messrs, ironmongers D54
Savage, John A3
Savings Bank R66
Savory & Moore, chemists D53
Sawyers, H R80
Sayers, Mrs, grocer, South St A10
Sayers, Joseph A13
<u>Scent maker</u>, Robert Best Ede A7, A17
Schools R54-61
  Academy R13
  John Box D50-51
  Church St Dames' R58
  Miss Cobden and Miss Mitchell A11
  Convent D20
  Dames R58
  East St R61
  Falkland D49
  Miss Gilliams Dames school A4
  Hampstead Lane R10
  High School A15
  Powell Corderoy (formerly British School) D10, D11, D33, D34, D50
  Royal British Schools R58
  Miss Stent and Miss Sumner A9
  Tower Hill D9
  Mr Wills A11
Scoble, John R28
Scott, Robert D5
Scott Hudson A13
Second Nower D24

Memories of Old Dorking

Seeboard A1, A9
Select Vestry R42
<u>Sewing machine agent</u>,
  Mr Girling D41
Shaw, Mr, coachman R72
Shearburn, Capt A19
Shearburn, Mr, South
  St A10
Shearburn, Mr G A21
Shearburn, William
  D32-3
Shearburn, Mr W A11
Shearman, Agnes A21
Shearman, Charlie D27-8
Sherlock, Mr A21
Sherlock, Messrs,
  coachbuilders A13
<u>Shoe shops</u>:
  Fred Lee D40
  Mr Marshall, High St
    A6
  Mr Warner, High St A7
<u>Shoemakers</u>, Mr Roomes
  R111
Shrub Hill R28, R66,
  R114, A4, D51
Shrub Hill estate A4
Shrub Hill mansion R10
Simmonds, Mr, printer
  D47
Sims, Mr, watcher R107
Singer machine shop D55
Singer Sewing Machine
  Company D41
Sirrons Employment
  Agency A8
Skilton, John ('Blind
  John') D38-9
Skilton, Richard A9
Skipper, Mrs, South St
  A9
<u>Slaughter house</u> R14,
  R84, D36
Slipper, Mr, cobbler,
  West St A15
Smith, Mrs, harness-
  maker A13
Smith, Bill R83
Smith, Mr G A20
Smith, W H & Sons A2,
  D48

<u>Soap factory</u>, Back Lane
  R19
Society of Friends R10,
  R85, R91, D1, D6, D39
  <u>see also</u> Friends
  Meeting House
<u>Solicitors</u>:
  Down, Scott & Down
    D10
  High St R28
  Hart & Sons A5
  Mr Martin, High St A6
Sondes, Earl of A14
Sondes Place (now the
  Vicarage) R11, A14
South St R2, R6, R8-10,
  R30, R59, R86, Ai,
  A11-12, A16, A20, D8,
  D13, D17, D23, D28,
  D32-46, D40
South Terrace Di, D1
Southease House D21
Spencer, Herbert D30
Spittal Heath A19
Spokes, Thomas A2
Spotted Dog R32, A9,
  D42
Spratley, Miss, toy and
  news shop, South St
  A12
Spratley, Mr D40
Spratley, Mr, High St
  A2
Spratley, Mr, stationer
  and newsagent D44
Spratley, Mrs, White
  Lion A8
Spratley, Robert, barber
  D43
Spratley, china and
  crockery shop, High St
  A2
Spring Gardens R6, D45,
  D53
Spurgeon, Rev Chas H
  D44
Squire, Misses, 'Wood-
  hurst' D1
'Stapleton', South St
  A12
Stapleton House R33,
  D21, D39, D40

Index

Star, the see Bell, the (formerly the Star)
Station Rd (formerly Washway) R13, D22, D45, D53
Stationers, Mr Spratley D44
Stations see Railway Stations
Statuary Showroom, Gilliam & Son's A15
Steer, Mr, gardener R43
Stent, Miss, schoolmistress R59, A9
Stent, Thomas A15
Stephenson, George R115
Stiff, Rev Neville G D1, D42
Stillwell, John G A11
Stitson, Mr, manager of Butters grocers D13
Stock Market R69-70
Stocks, the R2
Stone, Mr W A21
Stone & Turner, Messrs A7, A21
Stonemasons:
  Mr Gilliam, High St A4
  Mr Woodland D4
Stonestreet, George R40, R95
Stratton, Mr, West St A14
Stringer, Mr, gardener D17
Strudwick, Laura A21
Sturdy, Rev H C A19
Sturgeon, Mr, West St A14
Sumner, Miss, schoolmistress R59, A9
Sumner, Mr, parliamentary candidate R99, R100
Sun, the A2-3, D49
Sun Brewery R26
'Sunday at Home' D15
Surgeons:
  John Adee Curtis A9
  see also Doctors

Surrey Yeoman Inn R28, R63, R71, A5, D50, D51
Surrey Yeomanry Cavalry R10, R29
Surveyor, Frederick Muggeridge A9
Sweetheart's Lane (St Paul's Rd) R7
Sweet shops:
  Mrs Crompton D55
  West St R12
Swift, Mr, Three Tuns Hotel D36
Swiss Cottage R95

Tailors:
  W Beckett, High St A8
  High St A3
  Mr Joyce D45
  R Palladine, South St A8
Tallow chandlers:
  William Cheesman A3
  Beetham Wilson A7
Tanners, the printers A9
Tanners:
  Matthew Blaker A2
  High St A27
Tarling's Music Shop A13
Taylor, Mrs Elizabeth (née Watford) R32, R95, R96, R98
Taylor, James A9
Tea specialists, William Hollier D56
Tea and tobacco salesman, Charlie Shearman D27-8
Tebb Bros, clothiers D46
Temperance Hotel A14
Tenements, High St A1-2
Tesco A3
'Thirlstane' D10
Thompson, Thomas R41-2
Thorn, Mr 'Edgecombe' D14, D19
Three Tuns Club R64
Three Tuns Inn R26, R77, A3, D49

Memories of Old Dorking

Timber merchants,
  Brookers Di
Timbs, John, author of
  Promenade around
  Dorking R24, R44,
  R62, R92-3, R96, R98,
  R116
Tithe Barn A10
Tobacconist, G M Borer,
  High St A8
Todman, James D26
Todman, Miss N, organist
  D6
Toll bars/gates D27
  Harrow R7
  West St R13
    see also Paygates;
    Turnpikes
Toll keeper's cottage
  D27
Tooley, Mrs, dressmaker,
  South St A12
Tooley, George A12
Tower Hill R7, Di, D1,
  D2, D8
Tower Hill Rd D2, D10
Tower Hill School D9
Tower House D8-9
Town Brass, Drum and
  Fife Bands A19
Town Crier R41, D36
Town Hall A14
  see also Council
  Offices
'Townfield' A11, D30-31
Toy shops:
  Miss Agate D54
  Miss Isard, High St A7
  Miss Spratley, South
  St A12
Tracey, F F, butcher
  D36
Tracy, Mr, shopkeeper,
  South St A10
Trellis Cottage A10
Trimmer, Robert A2
Trollope, Mr, Holder
  House, South St A12
Tugwell, Mr, fishmonger
  D44
Tugwell, Mr, policeman
  D40

Turner, Mr H E A21
Turners and carpenters,
  High St R28
Turnpikes R105, R106,
  D3, D11, D12, D14,
  D29
    see also Paygates;
    Toll bars/gates

Undertakers:
  John Chart D48
  Frank Davey D50
  J Niblett A2
Union Bell D33
Union House R7, R34,
  R43, R65, R112
Union Workhouse D1
  see also Workhouse,
  the
United Reform Church Ri
Upfold, Thomas A9
Upholsterers:
  High St R25
  Mr Kendall D53
Upland Villas D17-18,
  D20
Usherwood, Mr D49-50
Utterton, Canon D17
Utterton, Miss, Upland
  Villas D17
Uwins, Mr R82
Uwins, Jnr, Mr, music
  shop, High St A7
Uwins, Richard A7

Verner, Mr W A20
Veterinary surgeons:
  Richard Finch, 'Lord
  Finch' R3
  Mr Howard, High St A3
Vicarage R35, R43
  North St R18-19
  Vincent's Lane R8
Vicarage (formerly
  Sondes Place) R11, A14
Victoria, Queen of
  England A7
Victoria Terrace A12,
  D40
'Viewlands' D25-6
Villa Building Co Aii
Vincent Drive D33

Index

Vincent's Lane R7, R8, R35, D33, D38
Vincent's Rd R7, D37
Vincent's Walk (formerly Cat's Fields Alley) R12, R33
Volckeryck, Rev Father A20, D20
Voluntary Fire Brigade D44, D48, D55

Walker, Mr, coach builder A4, D50
Walker, Mr, coachman R72
Walker, Mr, soapmaker R19
Walker, Edward A10
Walker, Israel R78
Walker, Mr J A20
Walker, Joseph R77-8
Walters, Mrs, South St A10
War Memorial A12
Ward, High St A7
Ward & Niblett A7
Warehouses:
   West St A13
    see also Furniture warehouse
Warner, Mr, bootshop, High St A7
Washway _see_ Station Rd
Washway, the _see_ Pipp Brook
Washway Bridge R13
Watchmakers:
   High St R24-5, R28, A6
   Thomas Hubbard A2
   Thos Hubbard Jnr A7
   Samuel Reeves A14
Watchman R39-40
Waters, Old Billy R63
Waterworks R19, D2
Watford, Mrs, tenant of the Hole-in-the Wall R93, R94, R97
Wathen, Capt R77, R113-14

Wathen, Lady Elizabeth Jane (née Leslie) R10, R29, R66, R77, R113-14, D51
Wathen Estate D50
Wathen Rd A4, D50
Weaver, High St R28
Webb, J Ogram, missioner D6, D8
Websters Bookshop A9
Weller, Mr, Presbyterian elder R51
Weller, Mr, shopkeeper, West St A14
Wellington, Duke of R108
Wellman, Thomas A3
Wells, Fred R80
Wells, James A9
Wesley, Rev John R14, A14, A16
Wesleyan Chapel R19, A11
Wesleyan schoolroom D36
West, Mr H A20
West St R3, R6, R11-18, R36, R46, R50, R61, R63, R84, R109, R110, Ai, A12, D5, D55-6
West St Antiques A14
West St Chapel A13
Westcott Borough R36
Westcott Mill A10, A16
Westcott Rd R11
Westland, Robert A4
Whaley, Mr A20
Whaley, Walter D42
Wheatsheaf Inn R6, R24, R67, R112, A1, A3
Wheelwrights:
   Vincent's Walk R33
   West St R12
White, Miss, schoolmistress R59
White, Misses, Upland Villas D17
White, Mr, builder, High St A3
White, Mr, grocer, High St A5
White, Mrs, homeopathic chemist D55
White, George A15

Memories of Old Dorking

White, Mr J A A21
White, James R25, R38-9
White Hart Inn R76
White Horse Hotel (formerly Inn) R4, R27, R101, A5-6, D53,
White Lion R30, A8, D45
White & Sons' A2
White & Sons, estate agents (formerly Alexander and Archibald White) D17, D49
White's, High St A2, A6
Whitehouse, Rev John R53, D43
Whitehouse, Mrs (widow of Congregational Minister) A12
Whitesmith, Mr Gittins A5
Whittle, Robert (Little Bob) R78
Wickham & Son A8
Wickman, Mr, confectioner D45
Wicks, Mr, lamplighter R6
Williams, Mary Sarah see Dinnage, Mary Sarah Di
Williams, William R15
Wills, Mr, schoolmaster A11
Wilson, Mr, barber D43
Wilson, Mr, chemist D53
Wilson, Beetham A7
Windmill Inn D11
Wine & spirit stores:
  Mrs Cheesman, South St A9
  High St R25
  Kingham & Co A7
  Joseph Maybank D47-8
Wood, Mr, landlord of the Duke's Head, Bear Green R23
Wood, Thomas D48
'Woodcote' D2, D10, D12
'Woodgate' Di
Woodger, Mr, muffin and crumpet seller R5
'Woodhurst' D1

Woodland, Mr, stonemason D4
'Woodlands' D2
Woodman, Mr Capon D19
Woodroffe, Joseph A8, A18
Woolworths D50
Wootton, Woodreeve R87
Workhouse R2, R33-4, R43, A10, D29, D33
  see also Union Workhouse
Working Men's Club D47
Working Men's Institute R62
Worley, E R80
Worley, Edward A7
Wotton estate R113
Wotton Hatch R102
Wotton, Hundred of R38
Wright, Thomas R72-3
Wyngate House D42
Wyngates, South St A12

Young, Capt, Rifle Volunteers A19
Young, Mr, brewer, Church St A16
Young, Mr, brick maker A17
Young, Mr, maltster A16
Young, Mr, Stapleton House D21
Young, Harman D21
Young, Heathfield R88
Young, John D39
Young Men's Christian Association R62
Young Men's Friendly Society A19
Young's Brewery D45